First World War

and Army of Occupation

War Diary

France, Belgium and Germany

48 DIVISION
Divisional Troops
475 South Midland Field Company Royal Engineers
29 March 1915 - 31 October 1917

WO95/2751/2

The Naval & Military Press Ltd
www.nmarchive.com
Published in association with The National Archives

Published by

The Naval & Military Press Ltd

Unit 10 Ridgewood Industrial Park,

Uckfield, East Sussex,

TN22 5QE England

Tel: +44 (0) 1825 749494

www.naval-military-press.com

www.nmarchive.com

This diary has been reprinted in facsimile from the original. Any imperfections are inevitably reproduced and the quality may fall short of modern type and cartographic standards.

Contents

Document type	Place/Title	Date From	Date To
Heading	WO95/2751/2		
Heading	48th Division 1-2nd S.M. Fld Coy R.E. Became 475th S.M. Fld Coy R.E. May 1915-Oct 1917		
Heading	48th Division 1/2 S.M. Field Coy R.E. Vol I 29.3.-15.15 Mar 19		
War Diary	Braintree Essex	29/03/1915	29/03/1915
War Diary	Southampton	30/03/1915	30/03/1915
War Diary	Havre	31/03/1915	01/04/1915
War Diary	Cassel (Bavinchove)	02/04/1915	02/04/1915
War Diary	Aux Trois Rois	02/04/1915	05/04/1915
War Diary	Coq de Paille	06/04/1915	07/04/1915
War Diary	Ploegsteert	08/04/1915	02/05/1915
Heading	48th Division 1/2nd S.M. Field Coy R.E. Vol II 1-31.5.15		
War Diary	Ploegsteert	01/05/1915	31/05/1915
Heading	48th Division 1/2nd S.M. Field Coy R.E. Vol III 1-30.6.15		
War Diary	Ploegsteert	01/06/1915	25/06/1915
War Diary	Bailleul	25/06/1915	26/06/1915
War Diary	Vieux Berquin	26/06/1915	27/06/1915
War Diary	Berguette	28/06/1915	28/06/1915
War Diary	Cauchy A La Tour	28/06/1915	30/06/1915
Heading	48th Division 1/2nd South Midland Field Coy R.E. Vol IV		
War Diary	Cauchy A-La-Tour	01/07/1915	10/07/1915
War Diary	Noeux-Les-Mines	10/07/1915	16/07/1915
War Diary	Couchy-A-La-Tour	17/07/1915	19/07/1915
War Diary	Doullens	19/07/1915	19/07/1915
War Diary	Beauquesne	20/07/1915	21/07/1915
War Diary	Courcelles	22/07/1915	31/07/1915
Heading	48th Division 1/2 S.M. Field Coy Vol V From 1-31.8.15		
War Diary	Courcelles	01/08/1915	31/08/1915
Heading	48th Division 1/2 S.M. Field Coy R.E. Vol VI Sept 15		
War Diary	Courcelles	01/09/1915	07/09/1915
War Diary	Sailly-Au-Bois	08/09/1915	30/09/1915
Heading	48th Division 1/2 S.M. Fd Co. R.E. Oct 15 Vol VII		
War Diary	Sailly-Au-Bois	01/10/1915	31/10/1915
Heading	48th Division 1/2nd Sth Midland Fd Co R.E. Nov 1915 Vol VIII		
War Diary	Sailly-Au-Bois	01/11/1915	30/11/1915
Heading	1/2nd S.M. Fd Co R.E. Dec Vol IX		
War Diary	Sailly-Au-Bois	01/12/1915	31/12/1915
Heading	1/2 S.M. Fd Co R.E. Jan Vol X		
War Diary	Sailly-Au-Bois	01/01/1916	31/01/1916
Heading	1/2 S M Fd Coy R.E. Feb Vol XI		
War Diary	Sailly Au Bois	01/02/1916	14/02/1916
War Diary	Rossignol Farm Coigneux	15/02/1916	29/02/1916
Heading	1/2 S M Fd Coy R.E. Vol XII		
War Diary	Rossignol Farm Coigneux	01/03/1916	02/03/1916

War Diary	Souastre	03/03/1916	31/03/1916
Heading	1/2 S M Fd Coy R.E. Vol XIII		
War Diary	Souastre	01/04/1916	05/05/1916
War Diary	Hem	06/05/1916	27/05/1916
War Diary	Rossignol Farm Coigneux	28/05/1916	12/06/1916
War Diary	Bivouac Near Sailly	13/06/1916	04/07/1916
War Diary	Rossignol	05/07/1916	13/07/1916
War Diary	Albert	14/07/1916	23/07/1916
War Diary	Bouzincourt	24/07/1916	25/07/1916
War Diary	Lealvillers	26/07/1916	27/07/1916
War Diary	Beauval	28/07/1916	28/07/1916
War Diary	Cramont	29/07/1916	31/07/1916
Heading	48th Divisional Engineers 1/2nd South Midland Field Company R.E. August 1916		
War Diary	Cramont	01/08/1916	07/08/1916
War Diary	Longvillers	08/08/1916	08/08/1916
War Diary	Authieule	09/08/1916	09/08/1916
War Diary	Acheux	10/08/1916	12/08/1916
War Diary	Aveluy	13/08/1916	31/08/1916
Heading	48th Divisional Engineers 1/2nd S.M. Field Coy Royal Engineers September 1916		
Heading	War Diary Of 1/2nd S.M Field Co R.E. 48th Div From 1st September 1916 To 30th September 1916		
Heading	War Diary Of 1/2nd (South Midland) Field Company R.E. 48th Division From 1st October 1916 To 31st October 1916		
War Diary	Authie	01/09/1916	10/09/1916
War Diary	Hem	11/09/1916	17/09/1916
War Diary	Outrebois	18/09/1916	23/09/1916
War Diary	Bernaville	24/09/1916	28/09/1916
War Diary	Caumesnil	29/09/1916	03/10/1916
War Diary	Henu	04/10/1916	20/10/1916
War Diary	Warlincourt	21/10/1916	24/10/1916
War Diary	Franvillers	25/10/1916	25/10/1916
War Diary	Mametz Wood	26/10/1916	31/10/1916
Heading	War Diary Of 1/2nd South Midland Field Coy R.E. 48th Division From 1st November 1916 To 30th November 1916 (Ops 56-57)		
War Diary	Mametz Wood	01/11/1916	04/11/1916
War Diary	Shelter Wood Valley	05/11/1916	30/11/1916
Heading	War Diary Of 1/2nd (S.M.) Field Company R.E. From 1st December 1916 To 31st December 1916 Vols		
War Diary	Shelter Wood Valley	01/12/1916	14/12/1916
War Diary	Bazentin Le Petit	15/12/1916	31/12/1916
Heading	War Diary Of 1/2nd (South Midland) Field Company R.E. From 1st January 1917 To 31st January 1917		
War Diary	Bazentin Le Petit	01/01/1917	31/01/1917
Heading	War Diary Of 475th (S.M.) Field Company R.E. For Month Of February 1917		
War Diary	Frise	01/02/1917	28/02/1917
Heading	War Diary Of 475th (S.M) Field Company R.E. For Month of March 1917-Pps 64 To 67		
War Diary	Frise	01/03/1917	21/03/1917
War Diary	Halle	21/03/1917	31/03/1917
Heading	War Diary Of 475th (S.M.) Field Company R.E. For Month Of April 1917 Pps 68-69		

War Diary	Peronne	01/04/1917	08/04/1917
War Diary	Villers Faucon	09/04/1917	12/04/1917
War Diary	St Emilie	13/04/1917	18/04/1917
War Diary	Ronssoy	19/04/1917	30/04/1917
Heading	War Diary Of 475th (S.M.) Field Coy R.E. For Month Of May 1917 Pps 70-71		
War Diary	Ronssoy	01/05/1917	01/05/1917
War Diary	St Emilie	02/05/1917	02/05/1917
War Diary	Peronne	03/05/1917	11/05/1917
War Diary	Le Mesnil	12/05/1917	12/05/1917
War Diary	Fremicourt	13/05/1917	13/05/1917
War Diary	Beugny	14/05/1917	19/05/1917
War Diary	Le Bucquiere	20/05/1917	31/05/1917
Miscellaneous	CRE 48th Division		
War Diary	Lebucquiere	01/06/1917	30/06/1917
Heading	War Diary Of 475th (S.M.) Field Company R.E. For Month Of July 1917		
War Diary	Lebucquiere	01/07/1917	01/07/1917
War Diary	Achiet Le Petit	02/07/1917	05/07/1917
War Diary	A 24d 11	06/07/1917	07/07/1917
War Diary	A 30a	08/07/1917	08/07/1917
War Diary	L Camp	09/07/1917	12/07/1917
War Diary	Camp At A21a 87	12/07/1917	31/07/1917
Heading	War Diary Of 475th (South Midland) Field Coy R.E. (T.F.) From 1st August 1917 To 31st August 1917		
War Diary	Vlamertinghe	01/08/1917	05/08/1917
War Diary	Canal Bank	07/08/1917	08/08/1917
War Diary	C 25 0 14	08/08/1917	14/08/1917
War Diary	Canal Bank	15/08/1917	15/08/1917
War Diary	Bund	16/08/1917	31/08/1917
Heading	War Diary Of 475th (South Midland) Field Company R.E. (Volume 30)		
War Diary	Bristol Farm	01/09/1917	01/09/1917
War Diary	H 10c76	01/09/1917	07/09/1917
War Diary	Bristol Farm	10/09/1917	27/09/1917
War Diary	Canal Bank	28/09/1917	30/09/1917
War Diary	Strength of Company Week Ending	07/09/1917	16/09/1917
War Diary	Canal Bank	18/09/1917	20/09/1917
Heading	War Diary Of 475th (South Midland) Field Co. R.E. From 1st October 1917 To 31st October 1917 (Volume 31)		
War Diary	Canal Bank	01/10/1917	10/10/1917
War Diary	A 22a55	14/10/1917	19/10/1917
War Diary	Aux Rietz	20/10/1917	31/10/1917

48TH DIVISION

BEF

1-2ND S.M. FLD COY R.E.
BECAME
475TH S.M. FLD COY R.E.

MAY 1915 - ~~MAR 1919~~ Oct 1917

To ITALY

48th Division

121/5254

1/2 S. M. Field Coy RE.

Vol I. 29.3 — 1.5.15

1

Mar '19

475th.

WAR DIARY

or

~~INTELLIGENCE SUMMARY.~~ 1/2 South Midland Field Co R.E.

(Erase heading not required.)

Instructions regarding War Diaries and Intelligence Summaries are contained in F. S. Regs., Part II. and the Staff Manual respectively. Title pages will be prepared in manuscript.

Army Form C. 2118.

1

Place	Date	Hour	Summary of Events and Information	Remarks and references to Appendices
BRAINTREE ESSEX	1915 March 29	6.0pm 7.30pm	Company left in two parts by march route for CHELMSFORD arriving 10.0 p.m. & 11.30 p.m. respectively. Men complained that new Army boots (which had been carefully fitted) made them very footsore altho' they have recently completed longer marches in boots supplied by the Gloucester County Association.	
			Entrainment of half companies with wagons & horses occupied 45 & 40 minutes respectively	
SOUTHAMPTON	30	7.0am 9.0am	Half companies arrived. All horses & wagons & 70 men + 4 officers embarked on S S MATHERAN, 120 men & 2 officers on S.S. MUNICH	
		7.30pm	S.S MATHERAN left	
		9.0pm	S.S. MUNICH left	
HAVRE	31	6.0am	S.S MUNICH arrived & men disembarked	
		10.0am	S.S MATHERAN arrived & disembarkation completed 4.30 pm. Tool cart wagon & G.S. wagon damaged in unloading & were replaced by A.O.D. Watercart pump cylinders also cracked in transit.	
			Company billeted for the night in Shed R at the Docks.	
	April 1	6.0am	Company arrived at Gare des Marchandises & entrained	
		10.0am	Train left	
CASSEL (BATINCHOVE)	2	6.30am	Arrived - during the night there was considerable trouble with the horses, a large number falling - in one truck 3 out of 4 fell & remained down for 2 hours; one being damaged & left at St. OMER	
AUX TROIS ROIS	2-5		Billeted in farms & rested - horses showed considerable signs of exhaustion after train journey	
	5	10.0am	Proceeded by march route to COQ de PAILLE - 1 kil N of FLETRE distance 22 km	
COQ de PAILLE	6		Billeted in farms	
	7		One horse died - apparently result of train journey this being one of the above 3 which were down for 2 hours	

1577 Wt. W10791/1773 500,000 1/15 D. D. & L. A.D.S.S./Forms/C. 2118.

Instructions regarding War Diaries and Intelligence Summaries are contained in F. S. Regs., Part II. and the Staff Manual respectively. Title pages will be prepared in manuscript.

WAR DIARY

~~or~~

~~INTELLIGENCE SUMMARY.~~

(Erase heading not required.)

Army Form C. 2118.

2

Place	Date	Hour	Summary of Events and Information	Remarks and references to Appendices
COQ de PAILLE	7	1.0 pm	Left by march route & joined South Midland Infantry Brigade at Starting Point at 3.0 pm. Proceeded via BAILLEUL to PLOEGSTEERT for attachment to 9th Field Co R.E. 4th Divn. Billeted in 3 Farms	
PLOEGSTEERT	8	5.0 pm	4 sections night work - construction of trenches in second line of defence on Point 63.	
	9		ditto	
	10		ditto	
			ditto - Demolished large tower of ruined villa on Point 63 - Guncotton charge 56 lbs	
	11		Men rested	
	12		2 sections commenced placing 2 farms in second line in state of defence	
	13		2 sections on night work - completing trenches in second line	
	14		ditto	
	15		ditto	
	16		ditto - One squad employed on hutting & roadmaking with 40 civilians	
	17		ditto	
	18		ditto	
	19		Preparations made for joining up front line trenches - 300 yards to be closed by communication trenches - 2 day sections made up gabions & cut pickets; 2 night sections completing trenches in second line	
	20		ditto - proposed lines of trenches reconnoitred & marked out	
	21		ditto - night working party of 200 infantry employed in carrying gabions & pickets to barn in rear of firing line & filling sandbags	
	22		ditto - 2 reliefs of 200 infantry employed in simultaneously placing gabions & otherwise revetting parapets of all connecting trenches & digging commenced. Old communication trench reconnoitred & repairs commenced with working party of 200	
	23		Work continued - Work on front line proceeded slowly owing to the earth having to be carried by the parapet, the ground being much cut up by old trenches & shell holes full of water. Owing to difficulties of drainage parapet made 3 feet above ground.	

Instructions regarding War Diaries and Intelligence Summaries are contained in F. S. Regs., Part II. and the Staff Manual respectively. Title pages will be prepared in manuscript.

WAR DIARY
or
INTELLIGENCE SUMMARY.

(*Erase heading not required.*) 1/2nd South Midland Field Co RE

Army Form C. 2118.

3

Place	Date	Hour	Summary of Events and Information	Remarks and references to Appendices
	24		Day work continued on farm. Owing to there being relief night no working parties were available. 2 sections employed at night on improving work on new trenches.	
	25		Day & night work continued with same working parties – Remainder of Klls [illegible] demolished by guncotton. Screen 30 yards long of brushwood made & erected to cover road junction on line of approach visible from Messines tower. Sites for support trenches & new communication reconnoitred.	
	26		Ditto – parapet of front trenches completed to height of 3 feet. Progress on communication trench slow owing to necessity for long drain – 500 yards of trench & approx 1500 yards of drain completed in 3 nights	
	27		Ditto – 200 yards of fire trench on reserve line dug	
	28		Ditto – Enclosed work at T 6 c 6-7 (Belgium sheet 28 S W 1/10000) commenced with working party of 180 & 12 sappers	
	29		Day work continued by 1 section & half section on night work at T 6 c 6-7 with 180 working party. Being relief night, remainder rested	
	30		500 yards of communication trench commenced from LA PLUS DOUCE Farm & U 7 c 5-5. 400 yards of fire trench (reserve line) dug. Front line work continued. Avenue of approach by day reconnoitred & detailed notes for corrected map taken. New line of communication decided upon.	

1577 Wt. W10791/1773 500,000 1/15 D. D. & L. A.D.S.S./Forms/C. 2118.

Instructions regarding War Diaries and Intelligence Summaries are contained in F. S. Regs., Part II. and the Staff Manual respectively. Title pages will be prepared in manuscript.

WAR DIARY
or
~~INTELLIGENCE SUMMARY.~~

(*Erase heading not required.*) 1/2nd South Midland Field Co. R.E.

Army Form C. 2118.

4

Place	Date	Hour	Summary of Events and Information	Remarks and references to Appendices
PLOEGSTEERT	1915 May 1		1 Section on day work, making trench boards & designing new form of wire entanglement (knife rest pattern). 3 Sections on night work – completing connecting trenches in front line, communication trenches & work on second line of defence. Infantry working parties amounted to 1200. 300 yards new communication trench dug	
	2		Ditto – 400 yards ditto	

1577 Wt. W10791/1773 500,000 1/15 D. D. & L. A.D.S.S./Forms/C. 2118.

48th Division

121/55/3

1/2nd S. M. Field Coy: RE.

Vol. II 1 — 31. 5. 15

Army Form C. 2118.

Instructions regarding War Diaries and Intelligence Summaries are contained in F. S. Regs., Part II. and the Staff Manual respectively. Title pages will be prepared in manuscript.

WAR DIARY
or
~~INTELLIGENCE SUMMARY.~~

(*Erase heading not required.*) 1/2nd South Midland Field Co. R.E.

4

Place	Date	Hour	Summary of Events and Information	Remarks and references to Appendices
PLOEGSTEERT	1915 May 1		1 Section on day work making trench boards & designing new form of wire entanglement (knife rest pattern)	
			3 Sections on night work - completing connecting trenches in front line, communication trenches & work on second line of defences. Infantry working parties amounted to 1200.	
			300 yards new communication trench dug	
	2		Ditto 400 " ditto	
			Site for enclosed work surveyed at In den KRAAIENBERG Cabaret (T.6.c.6.6) with a view to reducing perimeter	Sheet 28 1/40000
	3		Ditto - enclosed work commenced on perimeter of 430 yards. &	
	4		Ditto - 200 yards new communication trench dug	
	5		Ditto	
	6		Ditto	
	7		Ditto - 200 yards new communication trench dug	
	8		Ditto - 150 yards of fire trench on second line in front of LA PLUS DOUCE farm commenced	
	9		Ditto	
	10		Ditto	
	11		Ditto - One section withdrawn from night work & employed on day work laying trench boards & cleaning up & draining communication trenches	

1577 Wt. W10791/1773 500,000 1/15 D. D. & L. A.D.S.S./Forms/C. 2118.

Instructions regarding War Diaries and Intelligence Summaries are contained in F. S. Regs., Part II. and the Staff Manual respectively. Title pages will be prepared in manuscript.

WAR DIARY
or
~~INTELLIGENCE SUMMARY.~~

(*Erase heading not required.*) 1/2nd South Midland Field Co R.E. 5

Army Form C. 2118.

Place	Date	Hour	Summary of Events and Information	Remarks and references to Appendices
	May 12		Ditto New communication trench from T 18a 8-9 to LA PLUS DOUCE sited & commenced length 600 yards. Water tested for by Norton Tube at Encampment KORTEPYP T 27a 6-4 but failed to find in sufficient quantity	
	13		Ditto - repair of roads T 17 b 0-6 to T 17 d 3-1 and T 27 b 8-0 to T 28 b 4-9 completed - Section in front line for which unit responsible extends to U 8a 6-4	Sheet 28 S.W. [illegible]
	14		Ditto - 300 yards new communication trench dug - work continued on incomplete communication trench in front line taken over from 9th Field Co.	
	15		Ditto - Communication from Hill 63 (T 18a 6-7) ~~approx~~ 3000 yards now practicable by day but not complete	
	16		Ditto	
	17		Ditto - site for enclosed work at LA PLUS DOUCE surveyed & traced - perimeter 100 yards	
	18		Ditto - work commenced on new enclosed work	
	19		Ditto - work begun on parados to new front trench in front line taken over from 9th Field Co	
	20		Ditto - two new communication trenches each 30 yards long in front line surveyed & marked	
	21		Ditto	
	22		Ditto	
	23		Ditto	
	24		Ditto - above communication trenches (20th) completed	

1577 Wt. W10791/1773 500,000 1/15 D. D. & L. A.D.S.S./Forms/C. 2118.

Instructions regarding War Diaries and Intelligence Summaries are contained in F. S. Regs., Part II. and the Staff Manual respectively. Title pages will be prepared in manuscript.

WAR DIARY
or
~~INTELLIGENCE SUMMARY.~~

(*Erase heading not required.*)

Army Form C. 2118.

1/2nd South Midland Field Co R E 6

Place	Date	Hour	Summary of Events and Information	Remarks and references to Appendices
	May			
	25		Ditto	
	26		Ditto	
	27		Ditto	
	28		Sections rested except one section on night work in front line	
	29		Ditto (27th) - sites for 4 supporting points to second line surveyed	
	30		Ditto – sites for 4 supporting points to front line surveyed	
	31		Ditto Work commenced on supporting points. Report made upon all sources of water supply in area allotted to the unit	

G. F. Eberle
Major
2 S.M. Field Co R.E.

48th Division

121/5829

1/2nd S.M. Field Coy: RE

Vol III 1—30.6.15.

Instructions regarding War Diaries and Intelligence Summaries are contained in F. S. Regs., Part II. and the Staff Manual respectively. Title pages will be prepared in manuscript.

WAR DIARY
or
~~INTELLIGENCE SUMMARY.~~

(Erase heading not required.) 1/2nd South Midland Field Co. R.E. 7

Army Form C. 2118.

Place	Date	Hour	Summary of Events and Information	Remarks and references to Appendices
PLOEGSTEERT	1915 June 1	1	2 sections on day work - improving communications & general work in front line	
			2 " " night - work continued on supporting points to front & second line	
	2		Ditto	
	3		Ditto	
	4		Ditto - wiring between supporting points commenced	
	5		Ditto	
	6		Ditto	
	7		Ditto - New system of reliefs by brigades instituted by G.O.C. front line being held by 2 Brigades with 2 Field Companies attached, third brigade & field company being in reserve. Field company in reserve being responsible for roads, hutting, water supply etc behind firing line. 143rd Brigade (Infantry) having extended its line to the right as far as PROWSE POINT - U 14 b 2-2 this company became responsible for all work in same area & took over same from 1st S.M. Field Co. R.E.	
	8		Work continued as above - new area examined & sites for dugouts for supporting Company at U 14 a 6-5 reconnoitred	
	9		Ditto - construction of dugout commenced	

1577 Wt. W10791/1773 500,000 1/15 D. D. & L. A.D.S.S./Forms/C. 2118.

Instructions regarding War Diaries and Intelligence Summaries are contained in F. S. Regs., Part II. and the Staff Manual respectively. Title pages will be prepared in manuscript.

WAR DIARY
or
~~INTELLIGENCE SUMMARY.~~
(Erase heading not required.) 1/2nd South Midland Field Co R E

Army Form C. 2118.

8

Place	Date	Hour	Summary of Events and Information	Remarks and references to Appendices
PLOEGSTEERT	1915 June 10		Ditto - supporting points & wiring practically completed	
	11		Company went into reserve with 143rd Infantry Brigade Work commenced on 20 huts to accommodate 2 companies at T18d 5-6 Site for well at T17 b 5-5 surveyed & commenced	
	12		Ditto - one section struck off works daily for instruction & pontoon & trestle bridging	
	13		Ditto	
	14		Ditto inspection by GOC Division	
	15		Company took over line from LE TOUQUET to PROWSE POINT from 7th Field Co R.E. - 2 sections of 70th Field Co attached for instruction	
	16		Work continued on new trenches in front line, second line supporting points & sap heads driven out to two craters formed by enemy mining in the BIRDCAGE at U 21 b 7-5 and U 22 c 1-6	Sheet 28 S.W.
	17		Ditto	
	18		Ditto - two listening shafts commenced at PALK VILLA & PICKET HOUSE at the BIRDCAGE	
	19		Ditto - great difficulty experienced at PICKET HOUSE owing to quicksand at 8 feet	
	20		Ditto - 70th Field Co left	
	21		Ditto - site for new supporting point at ST YVES (S.T. YVON) U15c 10-7	

Army Form C. 2118.

WAR DIARY
or
INTELLIGENCE SUMMARY.
(Erase heading not required.)

Instructions regarding War Diaries and Intelligence Summaries are contained in F. S. Regs., Part II. and the Staff Manual respectively. Title pages will be prepared in manuscript.

Place	Date	Hour	Summary of Events and Information	Remarks and references to Appendices
PLOEGSTEERT	22		Ditto - Shaft at PARK VILLA successfully pushed thro' quicksand ~~[illegible]~~	
	23		Ditto -	
	24		Ditto - Shaft at PARK VILLA sunk to 17 feet. Instructions received that 87th Field Co would take over line & stores - Captain of 87th Field Co taken over portion of line	
	25		87th Field Co arrived & took over - Major & other officers taken over line stores, maps & details of work in progress handed over	
BAILLEUL		9.30pm	Company left for BAILLEUL	
	26	1.0am	Arrived in billets 1½ miles south of BAILLEUL. Company attached to 143rd Infantry Brigade for the march, the 48th Divn [illegible] moving by Brigade formation	
		9.0pm	Left billets	
VIEUX BERQUIN	~~27~~	12.30pm	Arrived billets at Ferme LESAGE 1½ mile N.E of VIEUX BERQUIN, having marched with 143rd Inf Brigade	
	27	8.0pm	Left billets for starting point X roads 1 mile SSW of La COURONNE - joined Brigade & marched via MERVILLE - ST VENANT - GUARBEQUE - HAM-EN-ARTOIS to BERGUETTE - distance approx 18 miles. 1 man fell out	
BERGUETTE	28	5.30am	arrived	
		5.0pm	left for starting point - marched with Brigade via LILLERS - BURBURE - RAIMBERT to CAUCHY-a-la-TOUR	
CAUCHY-à-la TOUR		9.30pm	arrived in billets - 1 man fell out on march	
	29		rested	
	30		General inspection, cleaning carts & stores, grinding tools &c.	

G. F. Eberle [illegible] Major
1/2nd S M Field Co RE

48th Division

121
6357

1/2nd South Midland Field Coy RE.

Vol IV

Army Form C. 2118.

Instructions regarding War Diaries and Intelligence Summaries are contained in F. S. Regs., Part II. and the Staff Manual respectively. Title pages will be prepared in manuscript.

WAR DIARY
~~or~~
~~INTELLIGENCE SUMMARY.~~

(Erase heading not required.) 1/2nd South Midland Field Co R.E

10

Place	Date	Hour	Summary of Events and Information	Remarks and references to Appendices
CAUCHY A-LA-TOUR	1915 July 1		Routine work and pontoon training	
	2		do	
	3		do	
	4		do	
	5		do	
	6		do	
	7		Sappers engaged in practice attack near ALLOUAGNE with 143rd Infantry Brigade	
	8		Routine work & pontoon training	
	9		do - O C Company attended Divisional Tactical Exercise do - two Officers detailed to reconnoitre second line of defence	
	10		do do	
NOEUX-LES-MINES	11		Company marched by night to NOEUX-LES-MINES & billeted	
	12		Company ordered to proceed by night to LES BREBIS & take over from 3rd London Field Co	
	13	1230 am	Arrived LES BREBIS	
		1.10 am	Orders received that taking over was cancelled & unit to return at once to NOEUX-LES-MINES working new trenches to second line and IV Corps instructions	
	14		Officers & NCOs engaged on new trenches - 1200 infantry in 2 reliefs - very wet night & little work done Night work on trenches	
	15		Night work with same parties of infantry	
	16		Night march to COUCHY-A-LA-TOUR	
COUCHY-A-LA-TOUR	17	3.0am	arrived	
	18		rested	

Instructions regarding War Diaries and Intelligence Summaries are contained in F. S. Regs., Part II. and the Staff Manual respectively. Title pages will be prepared in manuscript.

WAR DIARY
or
~~INTELLIGENCE SUMMARY.~~
(*Erase heading not required.*)

Army Form C. 2118.

1/2nd South Midland Field Co R.E "

Place	Date 1915	Hour	Summary of Events and Information	Remarks and references to Appendices
	July 19	1.0am	Left COUCHY-à-la-TOUR & marched to BERGUETTE (10 miles) - entrained by side-loading in 2¼ hours	
DOULLENS		1.0pm	arrived & detrained - marched to BEAUQUESNE (7 miles) & bivouacked	
			rested	
BEAUQUESNE	20		Headquarters section & section vehicles less forage ~~carts~~ marched to AUTHIE	
	21	7.0pm	& attached to 3rd S.M. Field Co R.E	
		8.0pm	Remainder of Company marched to COURCELLES & bivouacked	
			Visited French Engineers & arrangements made for taking over	
COURCELLES	22		Officers taken over line by French Officers & line taken over	
	23		NCOs & men taken through fire & communication trenches & shown saps	
	24		1 Officer 1 NCO & 4 sappers left in trenches on duty	
			Fire trenches & communication further reconnoitred	
	25		Two sections ordered to AUTHIE to take over work of 3rd S.M. Field Co R.E consisting of felling & cutting timber in WARNIMONT wood.	
		2pm	2 Sections moved & bivouacked in wood	
	26		The route to trenches being thro' HEBUTERNE (3 miles from COURCELLES) 2 half-sections moved into dugouts at S. end of ~~Hebuterne~~ HEBUTERNE & situate at entrance to main communication trench. Work in trenches of chief importance found to be provision of water - thickening of fire parapets & drainage of communication trenches.	

1577 Wt. W10791/1773 500,000 1/15 D. D. & L. A.D.S.S./Forms/C. 2118.

Instructions regarding War Diaries and Intelligence Summaries are contained in F. S. Regs., Part II. and the Staff Manual respectively. Title pages will be prepared in manuscript.

WAR DIARY
or
~~INTELLIGENCE SUMMARY.~~
(Erase heading not required.)

Army Form C. 2118.

1/2nd South Midland Field Co R.E. 12

Place	Date	Hour	Summary of Events and Information	Remarks and references to Appendices
COURCELLES	July 27		Well commenced in copse close to front line trenches - estimated required depth 70-100', entirely being chalk. Levelling & drainage of communication commenced	
	28		Ditto	
	29		Ditto - Position at LA SIGNY FARM reconnoitred	
	30		143rd Brigade relieved by 144 Brigade which extended its line by taking over 500 yards on the right and 300 yds on the left. This company remained in the line with 144th Brigade	
	31		Routine work - 2 sections in wood at WARNIMONT WOOD still engaged in supplying logs for artillery emplacements & pickets for Corps line, consequently very little available for front line work	

C. F. Steele Major
1/2nd S.M. Fd Co R.E.

1577 Wt. W10791/1773 500,000 1/15 D. D. & L. A.D.S.S./Forms/C. 2118.

48th Division

121
6561

1/2 S.M. Field Coy

Vol V

From 1 - 31. 8. 15

48th Division

121/0561

1/2 S.M. Field Coy

Vol V

From 1 - 31. 8. 15

Instructions regarding War Diaries and Intelligence Summaries are contained in F. S. Regs., Part II. and the Staff Manual respectively. Title pages will be prepared in manuscript.

WAR DIARY
or
~~INTELLIGENCE SUMMARY.~~
(Erase heading not required.)

Army Form C. 21[illegible].

1/2nd South Midland Field Co R E

13

Place	Date	Hour	Summary of Events and Information	Remarks and references to Appendices
COURCELLES	1915 August 1		Great difficulty experienced by right battalion in getting water, having to carry by hand from the SUCRERIE two miles away. Well found at LA SIGNY, containing lift & force pump but requiring horses or engine to work	
	2		All roads in neighbourhood reconnoitred with view to erecting signposts	
	3		Torrential rain during day & night resulting in flooding of Lower trenches to a depth of 2 to 3 feet, few sumps having been put in by the French	
	4		Scheme of drainage involving bricking or flooring important trenches & fire line with frequent sumps & a main drain following the valley & running out to the front	
	5		Work on drainage continued by Divisional Cyclist Co - at present bricks only being used, no timber being available	
	6		Ditto	
	7		Ditto	
	8		Well in front line struck water at 60 feet. Subsidiary fire trenches & enclosed work about LUNETTE D'ABLAIN (in front of S.E. corner of HEBUTERNE) reconnoitred, sited & traced. First consignment of timber for trench boards arrived	
	9		Daily working parties of infantry detailed as follows: 50 carpenters at R.E. store COURCELLES to make trench boards 50 day & night at LA SIGNY 50 to clean up & brick communication trench ST. EXUPERY on right of sector	

1577 Wt. W10791/1773 500,000 1/15 D. D. & L. A.D.S.S./Forms/C. 2118.

Instructions regarding War Diaries and Intelligence Summaries are contained in F. S. Regs., Part II. and the Staff Manual respectively. Title pages will be prepared in manuscript.

WAR DIARY
or
~~INTELLIGENCE SUMMARY.~~

(Erase heading not required.) 1/2nd South Midland Field Co R.E

Army Form C. 2118.

14

Place	Date	Hour	Summary of Events and Information	Remarks and references to Appendices
COURCELLES	9	cont^d	150 to clean up & brick communication trenches VERCINGETORIX & DU GUESCLIN. 75 (two reliefs by night) to dig subsidiary line at LUNETTE D'ARLAIN	
		8-11 pm	Very heavy thunderstorm & torrential rain – trenches flooded & very little night work done. Much damage to trenches which fell in in many places due largely to French system of scooping out holes as shelters in parapet	
	10		Both sections employed as far as possible in getting rid of water & repairing trenches. Further working party of 100 detailed daily on defences of COLINCAMPS. Trenches sited & traced at COLINCAMPS	
		6 am	Work commenced	
		8 am	No 4 Section relieved at WARNIMONT wood by section from 2/1 S M Field Co RE & marched to COURCELLES	
			Draft of 33 men arrived without any notification, deficient of smoke helmets & with no iron rations or rations for tomorrow – which A.S.C. had unable to obtain any rations. The responsibility for this lack of organisation appears to rest with OC No 1 Territorial Base Depot, MADRILLET Camp, ROUEN. Draft included a mounted corporal & 5 drivers supernumerary to establishment & not required or asked for.	
			Night party employed on digging a drain from front line towards the German trenches	
	11		Work continued in draining & repairing trenches – working parties as above	

1577 Wt. W10791/1773 500,000 1/15 D. D. & L. A.D.S.S./Forms/C. 2118.

Instructions regarding War Diaries and Intelligence Summaries are contained in F. S. Regs., Part II. and the Staff Manual respectively. Title pages will be prepared in manuscript.

WAR DIARY
or
~~INTELLIGENCE SUMMARY.~~

(*Erase heading not required.*) 1/2nd S.M. Field Co R.E

Army Form C. 2118.

15

Place	Date	Hour	Summary of Events and Information	Remarks and references to Appendices
COURCELLES	12		Cleaning up & draining of communication trenches continued	
	13		do	
	14		do	
	15		do	
	16		do	
	17		do	
	18		do	
	19		do	
	20		do	
	21		do	
	22		do - well in front line completed	
	23		do - pumping of water from well at LA SIGNY to BOW ST OBSERVATORY finally got into working order	
	24		do	
	25		Two right sectors (E & F) of front line + COLINCAMPS taken over by 4th Division. Worked continued in remaining sectors	
	26		do - Work commenced with 300 Infantry on back part of JENA	
	27		Remaining sectors (G & H) taken over by 145th Inf. Brigade but work continued temporarily. O.C visited FONQUEVILLERS with G.O.C 143 Inf Bde & inspected French trenches which were good but required draining & strengthening parapets	
	~~28~~ 28		Sections rested - Officers visited French trenches to North of HEBUTERNE	
	~~29~~ 29		Further 200 Infantry for work on JENA (night & day) cleaning up & draining	

1577 Wt. W10791/1773 500,000 1/15 D. D. & L. A.D.S.S./Forms/C. 2118.

Army Form C. 2118.

WAR DIARY
or
~~INTELLIGENCE SUMMARY.~~

Instructions regarding War Diaries and Intelligence Summaries are contained in F. S. Regs., Part II. and the Staff Manual respectively. Title pages will be prepared in manuscript.

(Erase heading not required.) 1/2nd South Midland Field Co. R.E. 16

Place	Date	Hour	Summary of Events and Information	Remarks and references to Appendices
COURCELLES	29		One section employed on Report Centre Dugouts for General Staff. Two & half section on TRNA, half section in workshops. Two Officers & 2 NCOs of 152nd Field Co. attached for instruction.	
	30		Work continued as above. Attached Officers & NCOs visited front trenches	
	31		do.	

G. F. Church [illegible] Major
1/2 S.M. Fd Co R.E.

1577 Wt. W10791/1773 500,000 1/15 D. D. & L. A.D.S.S./Forms/C. 2118.

48th Division

121/6930

1/2 S.M. Field Coy R.E.

Vol VI

Sept 15

WAR DIARY
or
~~INTELLIGENCE SUMMARY.~~

(*Erase heading not required.*) 1/2nd South Midland Field Co R.E 17

Army Form C. 2118.

Instructions regarding War Diaries and Intelligence Summaries are contained in F. S. Regs., Part II. and the Staff Manual respectively. Title pages will be prepared in manuscript.

Place	Date	Hour	Summary of Events and Information	Remarks and references to Appendices
COURCELLES	1915 Sept. 1		Section Officers & NCOs reconnoitred trenches in front of FONQUEVILLERS with a view to taking over	
			Sections employed on report centre dugouts & work on JENA	
	2		Two sections cleaned up evacuated billets, moving by motor to FONQUEVILLERS	
	3		One section at HEBUTERNE vacated billet & returned to COURCELLES. Remaining section at COURCELLES employed on trenchboard making & carpentry	
	4		Section at FONQUEVILLERS occupied on making good & pumping Communication trench No 3 on left battalion front of No 3 Inf Brigade. repairing & clearing wells	
	5		do - preparation begun for move from COURCELLES to SAILLY - transfer of stores commenced	
	6		do	
	7		do Headquarters & 2 sections moved to SAILLY	
SAILLY-AU-BOIS	8		Work on BRASSERIE well at FONQUEVILLERS commenced	
	9		Transfer of stores completed Dugouts at LA HAIE for Brigade Headquarters taken over in unfinished state & work continued - also on Report Centre Dugouts	
	10		do	
	11		do - widening of road BAYENCOURT to LA HAIE commenced & working party detailed daily to dig for flints	
	12		do	

Army Form C. 2118.

WAR DIARY
or
~~INTELLIGENCE SUMMARY.~~
(*Erase heading not required.*) 2 South Midland Field Co. RE

18

Instructions regarding War Diaries and Intelligence Summaries are contained in F. S. Regs., Part II. and the Staff Manual respectively. Title pages will be prepared in manuscript.

Place	Date	Hour	Summary of Events and Information	Remarks and references to Appendices
SAILLY-AU-BOIS	Septr 13		Work continued at LA HAIE & Report Centre Trenchboarding & repair of wells continued at FONQUEVILLERS	
	14		do. do. – main line of defence at FONQUEVILLERS having been left unfinished by the French, line of defence reconnoitred & traced	
	15		Section at FONQUEVILLERS relieved by section from SAILLY	
	16		Work continued as above – wiring & loopholing of walls commenced on FONQUEVILLERS main defences: Enemy dropped 12 5.9 incendiary shells near billets at SAILLY but without doing material damage.	
	17		ditto ditto	
	18		ditto ditto	
	19		ditto ditto	
	20		ditto ditto	
	21		ditto ditto	
	22		ditto ditto – enemy put 12 5.9 incendiary shells into SAILLY – surplus stores & hut transferred to Divisional R.E. Store –	
	23		Work concentrated on Report Centre – two hours bombardment by our guns of enemy's trenches – enemy replied & put 21 ~~dozen~~ 5.9 incendiary shells into SAILLY	
	24		Work on Report Centre which was completed – wagon packed for move. 2½ hours wirecutting by our artillery – 7 or 8 3" shells put into SAILLY	
	25		Quiet day – only work at R E Store – guns again bombarded enemy trenches, no reply.	

1577 Wt. W10791/1773 500,000 1/15 D. D. & L. A.D.S.S./Forms/C. 2118.

Army Form C. 2118.

WAR DIARY
or
~~INTELLIGENCE SUMMARY.~~

Instructions regarding War Diaries and Intelligence Summaries are contained in F. S. Regs., Part II. and the Staff Manual respectively. Title pages will be prepared in manuscript.

(*Erase heading not required.*) 1/2nd South Midland Field Co R.E 19

Place	Date	Hour	Summary of Events and Information	Remarks and references to Appendices
SAILLY-AU-BOIS	Sept 26		Routine work	
	27		do - section relieved at FONQUEVILLERS	
	28		do	
	29		do - section lectured on reconnaissance work by R.E	
	30		do - 2 Section carried out reconnaissance scheme. O.C met G.O.C 143 Inf Brigade & sited small keep on SAILLY-FONQUEVILLERS road	

G. F. Ebsok
Major
1/2nd S.M. F. Co R.E

1577 Wt. W10791/1773 500,000 1/15 D. D. & L. A.D.S.S./Forms/C. 2118.

48th Division

121/7496

1/2 S.M. 7th Co. R.E.

Oct. 15

Vol VII

48th

Instructions regarding War Diaries and Intelligence Summaries are contained in F. S. Regs., Part II. and the Staff Manual respectively. Title pages will be prepared in manuscript.

WAR DIARY
or
~~INTELLIGENCE SUMMARY.~~

Army Form C. 21[illegible]

(*Erase heading not required.*) 1/2nd South Midland Field Co. R E

20

Place	Date	Hour	Summary of Events and Information	Remarks and references to Appendices
SAILLY-AU-BOIS	Oct. 1		Work at FONQUEVILLERS - new communication trench 240 yards long known as Fifth Avenue dug in centre of L sector New keep on SAILLY Road known as JUNCTION KEEP commenced 2 large dugouts or shelters 25'x9' commenced in orchards Draining, levelling & trenchboarding or bricking of trenches continued Construction of Company H.Q. dugouts at LA HAIE continued Working parties fluming digging & roadmaking	
	2		Ditto	
	3		Ditto - Section at SAILLY practised bridge bridging	
	4		Ditto - New bombproof shelter commenced for guard at HEBUTERNE end of SAILLY Horse shelter in rear of Report Centre commenced Parties practised Stretchers	
	5		Ditto -	
	6		Ditto - Guards made for all wells in use in SAILLY to prevent soiling of bucket bottoms	
	7		Ditto	
	8		Ditto - Fifth Avenue completed, drained & bricked	
	9.		Ditto - Section relieved at night Two keeps to be known as the Northern & Southern keeps in village of FONQUEVILLARS sited by B.G.C 143 Inf Brigade & G.S.O I. Approx perimeters respectively of these keeps are 400 yards & 1000 yards.	

1577 Wt. W10791/1773 500,000 1/15 D. D. & L. A.D.S.S./Forms/C. 2118.

Instructions regarding War Diaries and Intelligence Summaries are contained in F. S. Regs., Part II. and the Staff Manual respectively. Title pages will be prepared in manuscript.

WAR DIARY

~~or~~

~~INTELLIGENCE SUMMARY~~.

(Erase heading not required.) 1/2nd South Midland Field Co R.E 21

Army Form C. 2118.

Place	Date	Hour	Summary of Events and Information	Remarks and references to Appendices
SAILLY-AU-BOIS	1915 Oct 10		Work at FONQUEVILLARS continued - new work on Southern keep commenced. Sections at SAILLY rested	
	11		All works continued - new ~~brigade~~ switch in brigade line from JUNCTION KEEP to junction of brigade line on SOUASTRE road sited & traced - 500 yards long	
	~~12~~		new battalion reserve line in rear of existing line in L sector sited & traced - 700 yards long	
	12		Ditto - new works commenced at FONQUEVILLARS; one section on trench bridges	
	13		Ditto - party instructed in bombing at 143 Brigade Bomb School - 18 shells put into SAILLY	
	14		Ditto -	
	15		Ditto - ditto; 2 large shelters in village of FONQUEVILLARS completed	
	16		Ditto	
	17		Ditto - 180 shells sent into SAILLY & considerable damage done - various repairs executed	
	18		Ditto - one section trench bridging	
	19		Ditto - ditto	
	20		Ditto - ditto	
	21		Ditto section relieved	

Instructions regarding War Diaries and Intelligence Summaries are contained in F. S. Regs., Part II. and the Staff Manual respectively. Title pages will be prepared in manuscript.

WAR DIARY

or

~~INTELLIGENCE SUMMARY.~~

Army Form C. 2118.

(Erase heading not required.) 1/2nd South Midland Field Co R.E. 22

Place	Date	Hour	Summary of Events and Information	Remarks and references to Appendices
SAILLY AU BOIS	1915 Oct 22		Ditto – Section at SAILLY visited	
	23		Ditto –	
	24		Ditto – circular route thro' orchards at SAILLY cut & marked with sods of chalk – for use of troops if village shelled	
	25		Ditto	
	26		Ditto – Weather very wet	
	27		Ditto	
	28		Ditto	
	29		Ditto	
	30		Ditto	
	31		Ditto.	

G. F. Eberle

Major
Commanding 1/2nd S.M. Field Coy.
Divl. Engineers.

1577 Wt. W10791/1773 500,000 1/15 D. D. & L. A.D.S.S./Forms/C. 2118.

48th Division

121/7636

1/2nd Sth Midland Fd. Co. RE.

Nov 1915

Vol ~~XI~~ VIII

Instructions regarding War Diaries and Intelligence Summaries are contained in F. S. Regs., Part II. and the Staff Manual respectively. Title pages will be prepared in manuscript.

WAR DIARY
or
~~INTELLIGENCE SUMMARY.~~
(Erase heading not required.) 1/2nd South Midland Field Co RE.

Army Form C. 2118.

23

Place	Date	Hour	Summary of Events and Information	Remarks and references to Appendices
SAILLY-AU-BOIS	1915 November 1		Work in hand at FONQUEVILLERS	
			(1) SOUTHERN KEEP	
			(2) NORTHERN KEEP	
			(3) Construction of Bomb-proof bomb store commenced	
			(4) battalion reserve line in L Sector between HEBUTERNE & FONQUEVILLERS	
			(5) new keep at LE CALVAIRE sited & commenced	
			(6) drainage & revetting of front line & communication trenches	
			Work at LA HAIE	
			(1) Series of dugouts for Company Offices	
			(2) Installation of improved water supply - erection of staging, double bucket rope & pipes to fill 1000 gallon tank.	
			(3) Levelling & grading track to the farm from the W.	
			(4) Extension of the LA HAIE CUT communication trench from LA HAIE to JUNCTION KEEP on SAILLY - FONQUEVILLERS road	
			Work at BAYENCOURT	
			(1) Wiring of front trenches continued	
			WORK at SAILLY	
			(1) 2 large bomb-proof shelters for wounded constructed at R.A.M.C dressing station	
			(2) a second circular route to avoid shelling marked with white posts & gaps cut thro' orchards on Southern side of village, leading to JENA communication trench	
			(3) general work at RE Divisional Store including making concrete blocks & water troughs	
			WORK at ROSSIGNOL	
			(1) construction of stables	

1577 Wt. W10791/1773 500,000 1/15 D. D. & L. A.D.S.S./Forms/C. 2118.

Army Form C. 2118.

Instructions regarding War Diaries and Intelligence Summaries are contained in F. S. Regs., Part II. and the Staff Manual respectively. Title pages will be prepared in manuscript.

WAR DIARY
or
~~INTELLIGENCE SUMMARY.~~

(Erase heading not required.) 1/2nd South Midland Field Co RE

Place	Date	Hour	Summary of Events and Information	Remarks and references to Appendices
SAILLY-AU BOIS	Nov. 2		Ditto. Very heavy rain – trenches flooded Section relieved by night	
	3		Ditto – Rain continued	
	4		Ditto – weather improved Considerable falling in of unrevetted trenches Front line & communication trenches which had been systematically graded & drained stood the test well but a quantity of water & mud accumulated in others Section at FONQUEVILLERS employed night & day on pumping & cleaning	
	5		Ditto	
	6		Ditto – Trenchboarding of LA HAIE CUT commenced	
	7		Ditto –	
	8		Ditto –	
	9		Ditto –	
	10		Ditto – very heavy rain – unrevetted trenches falling in everywhere.	
	11		Ditto – ditto – L Sector opposite GOMMECOURT fairly good M Sector in front of FONQUEVILLERS suffered severely especially when Germans put in 60 Minenwerfer which assisted collapse of trenches	
	12		Ditto – working parties on night & day cleaning up & repairing trenches	

1577 Wt. W10791/1773 500,000 1/15 D. D. & L. A.D.S.S./Forms/C. 2118.

WAR DIARY
or
~~INTELLIGENCE SUMMARY.~~

(*Erase heading not required.*)

Army Form C. 2118.

Instructions regarding War Diaries and Intelligence Summaries are contained in F. S. Regs., Part II. and the Staff Manual respectively. Title pages will be prepared in manuscript.

1/2nd South Midland Field Co RE 25

Place	Date	Hour	Summary of Events and Information	Remarks and references to Appendices
SAILLY AU BOIS			Such portions of the front line & such communications as had been properly drained stood better than others even tho' not revetted	
	13		Ditto - weather improved enabling progress - all working parties transferred to the front line	
	14		Ditto - a fine day. GOMMECOURT heavily shelled by us section relieved.	
	15		Ditto	
	16		Ditto	
	17		Ditto	
	18		Ditto	
	19		Ditto	
	20		Ditto	
	21		Ditto	
	22		Ditto - weather continued fine to this date enabling condition of trenches to be much improved	
	23		Ditto - weather again bad	
	24		Ditto	
	25		Ditto	
	26		Ditto - hard frost set in - section relieved	
	27		Ditto	
	28		Ditto	
	29		Ditto - thaw & very heavy rain - further falls in the trenches but on the whole they survived remarkably well	
	30.		Ditto - a fine day enabling clearing of trenches to continue	

1577 Wt. W10791/1773 500,000 1/15 D. D. & L. A.D.S.S./Forms/C. 2118.

Instructions regarding War Diaries and Intelligence Summaries are contained in F. S. Regs., Part II. and the Staff Manual respectively. Title pages will be prepared in manuscript.

WAR DIARY

or

~~INTELLIGENCE SUMMARY.~~

(Erase heading not required.) 1/2nd South Midland Field Co RE

Army Form C. 2118.

26

Place	Date	Hour	Summary of Events and Information	Remarks and references to Appendices
SAILLY AU BOIS	1915 August		Summary of work during the month - FONQUEVILLERS (1) Southern Keep - New trenches completed & drained Wiring completed 5 M G emplacements constructed (2) Northern Keep = nearly completed (3) Bomb proof store completed (4) Brigade reserve line completed by 500 yards new trench (5) Keep at LE CALVAIRE nearly completed rewired, quite Revetted (6) Many sumps dug & revetting, trenches graded & drained & much work done in sloping back trenches & clearing the berm. Several dugouts (French) which had collapsed, repaired. Portion of front line boarded or bricked (7) SAILLY road trench graded & drained by 200 yards drains & boarded to JUNCTION KEEP LA HAIE (1) Dugouts for Company Officers completed Several dugouts repaired (2) Water supply completed (3) levelling of track from the W completed (4) LA HAIE CUT completely dug Trench boarding laid from junction of SAILLY-SOUASTRE & BAYENCOURT - LA HAIE roads to LA HAIE CUT - JUNCTION KEEP - FONQUEVILLARS - 3400 yards of boarding	

1577 Wt. W10791/1773 500,000 1/15 D. D. & L. A.D.S.S./Forms/C. 2118.

Instructions regarding War Diaries and Intelligence Summaries are contained in F. S. Regs., Part II. and the Staff Manual respectively. Title pages will be prepared in manuscript.

WAR DIARY
or
~~INTELLIGENCE SUMMARY.~~

(Erase heading not required.) 1/2nd South Midland Field Co RE

Army Form C. 2118.

27

Place	Date	Hour	Summary of Events and Information	Remarks and references to Appendices
			BAYENCOURT – wiring continued	
			SAILLY – (1) RAMC bomb proof shelter completed	
			(2) Second circular route completed	
			(3) usual general work at RE store	
			ROSSIGNOL – Stables completed	
			Following correspondence issued by C.R.E. –	
			1	
			" G.O.C. 48 Division	
			It has been brought to the notice of the Corps Commander that the Engineer services of your Division are particularly well carried out.	
			He has directed me to ask you to inform Colonel Marshall & those under his command that this report of their efficiency has given him much pleasure	
			F. Lyon Brig. Gen. 7th Corps	
			24.11.15	
			2	
			To Colonel Marshall	
			This report is I consider a result of your own & your assistants untiring work carried out often under very great difficulties. Please return after you have communicated the contents	
			R Fanshawe Major Gen. Commanding 48 Division	
			24.11.15	

1577 Wt. W10791/1773 500,000 1/15 D. D. & L. A.D.S.S./Forms/C. 2118.

G.F. Ch[illegible] Major 2 SM F Co RE

48

1/2nd S.M. Fd. Co. R.E.

Dec.

Vol IX

Instructions regarding War Diaries and Intelligence Summaries are contained in F. S. Regs., Part II. and the Staff Manual respectively. Title pages will be prepared in manuscript.

WAR DIARY
or
~~INTELLIGENCE SUMMARY.~~

(Erase heading not required.) 1/2nd South Midland Field Co. R.E.

Army Form C. 2118.

28

Place	Date	Hour	Summary of Events and Information	Remarks and references to Appendices
SAILLY AU BOIS	1915 December 1		Work in front line a FONQUEVILLERS devoted mainly to revetting & keeping open communication trenches & front line – weather very bad – many French dugouts fell in or became waterlogged uninhabitable. Work on CALVAIRE KEEP continued – also on LA HAIE CUT	
	2		Ditto	
	3		Ditto	
	4		Ditto	
	5		Ditto – 30 shells put into SAILLY	
	6		Ditto – 2 sections 202nd Field Co. R.E. attached for instruction & billeted at FONQUEVILLERS	
	7		Ditto	
	8		Ditto – 20 shells into SAILLY – section relieved	
	9		Ditto – 100 " " "	
	10		Ditto – CALVAIRE KEEP completed	
	11		Ditto – B.G.C. decides to abandon LA HAIE CUT	
	12		Ditto – alternative route (in lieu of LA HAIE CUT) reconnoitred – approx 200x S [illegible]	
	13		Ditto –	
	14		Ditto – trench boards begun to be recovered from LA HAIE CUT (very heavy work) & laid on new route	
	15		Ditto – 200 shell in & around SAILLY	
	16		Ditto	
	17		Ditto	
	18		Ditto – 202 Field Co left	
	19		Ditto	
	20		Ditto – section relieved	

5771 Wt. W10791/1773 500,000 1/15 D. D. & L. A.D.S.S./Forms/C. 2118.

Army Form C. 2118.

WAR DIARY
or
~~INTELLIGENCE SUMMARY.~~

Instructions regarding War Diaries and Intelligence Summaries are contained in F. S. Regs., Part II. and the Staff Manual respectively. Title pages will be prepared in manuscript.

(Erase heading not required.) 1/2nd South Midland Field Co RE

29

Place	Date 1915	Hour	Summary of Events and Information	Remarks and references to Appendices
SAILLY-AU-BOIS	December 20		Orders received to commence 5 saps or breastworks (2 in L sector 3 in M sector) - preliminary work started by clearing out existing saps at following points - J 3d-3-7½, J 3b 4-8, F 28c 2-7, F 28a 9-1, F 28b 3-9	
	21		Ditto - Shrapnel proof shelter begun along new route - ~~LA HAIE~~ CUT	
	22		Ditto	
	23		Ditto	
	24		Ditto	
	25		Ditto - 80 shells into SAILLY	
	26		Ditto	
	27		Ditto - work on saps stopped thro' shortage of men	
	28		Ditto	
	29		Ditto	
	30		Ditto	
	31		Ditto	
			Work during month consisted mainly in maintaining trenches & communication as far as possible by revetting, pumping &c., repairing dugouts & drainage. The soil in this part of the country becomes very unstable when thoroughly soaked & trenches to stand unrevetted require slope of 1/1 side.	

G. F. [illegible] Major
2 S M Fd Co RE

1577 Wt. W10791/1773 500,000 1/15 D. D. & L. A.D.S.S./Forms/C. 2118.

11

Army Form C. 2118.

WAR DIARY
or
~~INTELLIGENCE SUMMARY.~~

(Erase heading not required.) 1/2nd South Midland Field Company R E 30.

Instructions regarding War Diaries and Intelligence Summaries are contained in F. S. Regs., Part II. and the Staff Manual respectively. Title pages will be prepared in manuscript.

Place	Date	Hour	Summary of Events and Information	Remarks and references to Appendices
SAILLY-AU-BOIS	1916 Jan 1		Usual work continued – SAILLY Divisional RE Park shelled – 6 casualties & 2 horses killed	
	2		Ditto – site for artillery observation post & sunk telephone shelter selected by RAA	
			Memorandum issued by 143 Brigade to Battalions that time had now arrived when infantry should maintain their trenches & carry out the simpler forms of field engineering such as revetting & drainage without RE assistance & consequently sappers would not be used in the front trenches altho' RE Officers & NCOs would be available to give advice as required.	
	3		Sections released – one section only for Brigade requirements, the other being retained by CRE for construction of observation posts	
	4		Ground between FONQUEVILLERS Northern Keep & adjacent keep of 37th Division wired to a depth of 50 yards. Commenced work of observation post at LA CALVAIRE (M sector)	
	5		Ditto	
	6		2 Companies of 2 Battn Lancashire Fusiliers attached to 143 Inf Brigade for work only –	
	7		Working parties L F on breastwork at entrance to FONQUEVILLERS, barricade in main street, bombstore at the Brasserie, shrapnel proof shelter on the SAILLY-FONQUEVILLERS road, sandbag traverses in barns at LA HAIE	

Instructions regarding War Diaries and Intelligence Summaries are contained in F. S. Regs., Part II. and the Staff Manual respectively. Title pages will be prepared in manuscript.

WAR DIARY
or
~~INTELLIGENCE SUMMARY.~~

(*Erase heading not required.*)

Army Form C. 2118.

1/2nd South Midland Field Co. R.E. 31

Place	Date 1916	Hour	Summary of Events and Information	Remarks and references to Appendices
SAILLY AU BOIS	Jan 8		Work continued – 220 shells into SAILLY which was shelled 4 times	
	9		" – Route to the north of SAILLY marked by white posts – to enable troops to avoid SAILLY during shelling	
			Division decide to remove R.E. Park to COURCELLES	
	10		Orders received to prepare new store at COURCELLES and 8 men billeted there temporarily	
	11		G.O.C went round Brigade Area and inspected site of bomb stores – approved	
	12		scheme for screening troops moving from LA HAIE to FONQUEVILLERS	
	13		B.G.C sited new small post on extreme left of Brigade Reserve line	
	14		Brazenose bomb store, breastwork at entrance to village & barricade in main street completed	
	15		New work commenced at Artillery House FONQUEVILLERS, to be improved for defence – new M.G. positions sited & banquette & loop holes for fire commenced. One section moved from SAILLY to COURCELLES for duty at R.E. Park & workshops	
	16		Work continued. New Brigade Bomb Store commenced at LA HAIE – to hold 30000 grenades, heavy trench mortar bombs & large detonator room	
	17		do	
	18		do	
	19		do – new small post on left of Brigade Reserve Line completed & wired; sections relieved	
	20		do	
	21		do	
	22		do	
	23		do	
	24		do	

Army Form C. 2118.

Instructions regarding War Diaries and Intelligence Summaries are contained in F. S. Regs., Part II. and the Staff Manual respectively. Title pages will be prepared in manuscript.

WAR DIARY
or
~~INTELLIGENCE SUMMARY.~~

(Erase heading not required.) 1/2nd South Midland Field Co R.E

32

Place	Date	Hour	Summary of Events and Information	Remarks and references to Appendices
SAILLY-AU-BOIS	1916 JAN.	25	Worked continued – Heavy bombardment of L & M sectors by the enemy 2am to 2.30am	
		26	do	
		27	do – one observation post at LE CALVAIRE completed – Gas alarm received at 7.28 pm but proved to be false	
		28	do false gas alarm at 7.20 am	
		29	do – Proposed bombing attack on GOMMECOURT wood abandoned owing to fog.	
		30	do	
		31	do	

Summary of work during the month

FONQUEVILLERS – Strong post at ARTILLERY CROSS ROADS nearly completed
new barricade across main road in SOUTHERN KEEP
20 yards new breastwork on N. face of S. KEEP
40 yards new breastwork at Gorge of S. KEEP.
Battalion Reserve Bombstore at the Brasserie completed
Advanced Brigade " " ENTRANCE to village "
One artillery observation post with mined telephone shelter at LE CALVAIRE completed
Second ditto at LE CALVAIRE partially ~~complete~~ made
~~third~~ ditto in THORPE Street (L sector) partially made
new liaison trench L & K sector dug – 200 yards
new Battalion Reserve Bombstore constructed in bluff behind L Sector

Brigade Reserve Line – new strong post completed at extreme left of line
Shrapnel proof shelters (each to cover 12 men) constructed along avenues of approach viz
5 in Sunken road – LA HAIE to HEBUTERNE
6 on SAILLY – FONQUEVILLERS road between JUNCTION KEEP & VALLEY ROAD
6 on VALLEY ROAD

LA HAIE – New Brigade Bomb store partially built – several collapsed shelters repaired

G. F. Ebrook [?] Major
Comdg 1/2nd SM Field Co R.E.

1577 Wt. W10791/1773 500,000 1/15 D. D. & L. A.D.S.S./Forms/C. 2118.

48

1/2 S M Fd. Coy R. E.

Feb

Vol XI

Instructions regarding War Diaries and Intelligence Summaries are contained in F. S. Regs., Part II. and the Staff Manual respectively. Title pages will be prepared in manuscript.

WAR DIARY

or

~~INTELLIGENCE SUMMARY.~~

(*Erase heading not required.*) 1/2 South Midland Field Co RE

Army Form C. 2118.

33

Place	Date	Hour	Summary of Events and Information	Remarks and references to Appendices
SAILLY AU BOIS	1916 Feby 1		General work continued	
	2		do	
	3		do	
	4		do New observation post & covered shelter commenced at the MOULIN DETRUIT L Sector	
	5		do strong post at Artillery Cross Roads - FONQUEVILLERS completed.	
	6		do ~~second~~	
	7		do	
	8		do. Increased enemy artillery activity	
	9		do 30 shells into SAILLY	
	10		do - New trench tramway commenced - do drawn from X roads between BAYENCOURT - to H.Q. L Sector - total	
	11		do. & LA HAIE via LA HAIE JUNKER ROAD	
	12		do distance 4700 yards	
	13		do Northern part of FONQUEVILLERS	
	14		do H.Q. + 1 section left SAILLY - 1 section RE billeted there	
ROSSIGNOL FARM COIGNEUX	15		do taken over by 143 Inf. Brigade	
	16		do H.Q. removed to ROSSIGNOL FARM - COIGNEUX	
	17		do New artillery observation post commenced in Artillery House FONQUEVILLERS	
	18		do to consist of a square tower 30' high built inside the house	
	19		do second O.P. in LE CALVAIRE road completed	
	20		do	
	21		do	
	22		do	
	23		do	
	24		do	
	25		do	

1577 Wt. W10791/1773 500,000 1/15 D. D. & L. A.D.S.S./Forms/C. 2118.

Instructions regarding War Diaries and Intelligence Summaries are contained in F. S. Regs., Part II. and the Staff Manual respectively. Title pages will be prepared in manuscript.

WAR DIARY
or
~~INTELLIGENCE SUMMARY.~~

(Erase heading not required.) 1/2nd South Midland Field Co. R.E.

Army Form C. 2118.

34.

Place	Date	Hour	Summary of Events and Information	Remarks and references to Appendices
ROSSIGNOL FARM	1916 Feb.			
COIGNEUX	26		General work continues	
	27		do O P in Thorpe street completed	
	28		do	
	29		do	
			Summary of work during the month	
			FONQUEVILLERS – Strong point at Artillery Cross Roads completed	
			Second Artillery O P on LE CALVAIRE road completed	
			Artillery O.P. in Thorpe street on FONQUEVILLERS – HEBUTERNE road completed – ditto on same road at the MOULIN DETRUIT nearly completed	
			" Artillery O.P. tower commenced in Artillery House	
			New screened route between LA HAIE & FONQUEVILLERS practically complete – 250 yards of screening 3' & 6' erected	
			Brigade Bomb Store at LA HAIE practically complete	
			3400 yards of trench tramway laid	

G. F. Cheek[?]
Major
Comdt. 1/2nd S.M. Field Co
R.E.

1577 Wt. W10791/1773 500,000 1/15 D. D. & L. A.D.S.S./Forms/C. 2118.

48

1/2 S M 3rd Coy R.E.

Vol XII

Instructions regarding War Diaries and Intelligence Summaries are contained in F. S. Regs., Part II. and the Staff Manual respectively. Title pages will be prepared in manuscript.

WAR DIARY
or
~~INTELLIGENCE SUMMARY.~~
(Erase heading not required.) 1/2nd South Midland Field Co R.E.

Army Form C. 2118.

35

Place	Date	Hour	Summary of Events and Information	Remarks and references to Appendices
ROSSIGNOL FARM	1916 March		General work continued	
	1			
COIGNEUX	2		do	
SOUASTRE	3		do – Headquarters section & all transport moved from ROSSIGNOL to SOUASTRE One section moved from COURCELLES to SOUASTRE	
	4		do Sections relieved	
	5		do 143 Inf Brigade handed over Northern end of FONQUEVILLERS to	
	6		do. 37th Division – no of RE sections for front work accordingly reduced to two & one section returned to SOUASTRE O.P at MOULIN DETRUIT completed Both sections employed on building latrines, washing sheds for	
	7		do – SOUASTRE – & a certain amount of training in bridging & rapid wiring	
	8		do	
	9		do	
	10		do	
	11		do	
	12		do	
	13		do	
	14		do	
	15		do	
	16		do	
	17		do	
	18		do New screen route completed	
	19		do Trench tramway BAYENCOURT x roads to L sector complete except for 400 yds – stopped for lack of material	
	20		do	
	21		do Sections relieved	

Instructions regarding War Diaries and Intelligence Summaries are contained in F. S. Regs., Part II. and the Staff Manual respectively. Title pages will be prepared in manuscript.

WAR DIARY
or
~~INTELLIGENCE SUMMARY.~~

(*Erase heading not required.*) 1/2nd South Midland Field Co RE

Army Form C. 2118.

36

Place	Date	Hour	Summary of Events and Information	Remarks and references to Appendices
COUASTRE	1916 March 22		General work continued - Raid on enemy's trenches by 8 R War Regt - Bangalore torpedoes used to cut the wire with	
	23		do	
	24		do Bombstore for Brigade Reserve at LA HAIE completed - a new	
	25		do addition thereto by protecting an adjoining cellar commenced	
	26		do Cleaning & boarding of communication trench from Euston to FONQUEVILLERS	
	27		do 5 cross roads (Ashley X roads) commenced	
	28		do One section employed on hutting at COUIN	
	29		do	
	30		do	
	31		do	

Summary of work during the month

FONQUEVILLERS - O.P. at MOULIN DETRUIT completed - consists of a shaft 25' deep a 23' gallery & 8' x 6' shelter with an upward shaft to a Camouflage O.P.

Infantry sleeping post placed in front trenches near the GOMMECOURT Road

RAMC dressing shelters commenced & 50' completed

Ashley O.P. tower at Ashley House nearly completed

New screened route between LA HAIE & FONQUEVILLERS completed

1100 yds trench tramway laid

Brigade Bombstore at LA HAIE completed Euston to FONQUEVILLERS completed

Extension to forward Brigade Bombstore at Euston and trenches cleared & revetted

Wiring at FORT DICK strengthened

General work comprising making Bangalore torpedoes, folding beds, making up railway trollies, strengthening existing shelters, hutting etc.

[illegible] Major
2 S M Fd Co R.E.

1577 Wt. W10791/1773 500,000 1/15 D. D. & L. A.D.S.S./Forms/C. 2118.

48

1/2 S M 3d Coy R E

Vol XIII

Instructions regarding War Diaries and Intelligence Summaries are contained in F. S. Regs., Part II. and the Staff Manual respectively. Title pages will be prepared in manuscript.

WAR DIARY

or

~~INTELLIGENCE SUMMARY.~~

(Erase heading not required.)

Army Form C. 2118.

1/2nd South Midland Field Co R.E.

37

Place	Date	Hour	Summary of Events and Information	Remarks and references to Appendices
SOUASTRE	April 1		General work continued - SOUASTRE shelled	
	2		do do - party erecting water troughs at COUIN	
	3		do	
	4		do	
	5		do - new false roof to Brigade Office LA BAZÈQUE commenced	
	6		do	
	7		do	
	8		do - mined dugout near SAILLY for artillery shelter commenced by R.A. under RE supervision	
	9		Section at FONQUEVILLERS relieved by 1 section only One section moved to ROSSIGNOL to take over Divisional RE store Two sections at SOUASTRE	
	9		do	
	10		do - One section moved to VALHEUREUX for work at IV Army Trench Mortar School	
	11		do	
	12		do	
	13		do	
	14		do	
	15		do	
	16		do	
	17		do	
	18		do	
	19		do	
	20		do	
	21		do	
	22		do	
	23		do	
	24		do - Section at FONQUEVILLERS relieved	

Instructions regarding War Diaries and Intelligence Summaries are contained in F. S. Regs., Part II. and the Staff Manual respectively. Title pages will be prepared in manuscript.

WAR DIARY

or

~~INTELLIGENCE SUMMARY.~~

(*Erase heading not required.*) 1/2nd ~~South~~ Midland Field Co R.E.

Army Form C. 2118.

38

Place	Date	Hour	Summary of Events and Information	Remarks and references to Appendices
SOUASTRE	April 25		General work continued – erection of 4 huts for 1st [illegible] Field Amb. Hospital commenced. L sector taken over by 144 Inf Brigade + M sector with 1 Battn 143 Inf. Brigade attached	
	26		do	
	27		do – new strong point 100 yards W. of MOULIN DETRUIT sited & commenced	
	28		do	
	29		do –	
	30		do – RAMC hospital completed.	

Summary of work during month

FONQUEVILLERS – O.P at Hotchkiss House completed (ARTILLERY HOUSE O.P.)
Two O.P's each for two observers completed in M sector near front line
O.P in Brewery Orchard nearly completed
New communication trench & new fire position constructed in CENTRAL KEEP
New strong post at ARTILLERY CROSS ROADS completed & wired
New communication trench (300 yards) dug to 10th BRASSERIE
Trench & No 2 Communication Trench, running 100 west of main road
Belt of wire completed across village from CENTRAL KEEP to Western edge. – Rifleman fire position & 5 M.G. emplacements constructed to cover same
Dressing station shelters (120 feet in all) completed
Strengthening & thickening of roof to Advanced Brigade H.Q. commenced
New strong point near MOULIN DETRUIT (L sector) commenced
Wiring in front of SIXTH STREET (L sector) commenced

LA HAIE – False roof giving 2 feet extra cover to Brigade Office nearly completed
Protection of large cellar for use as detonating room & [illegible] nearly completed
Construction of new battery emplacements & shelters (for 4 guns) under RE supervision completed
Almost shelter for Artillery near SAILLY practically complete
One section at Divisional RE Store on general work including making beds, water troughs & hutting
4 Hospital huts (40'x20') erected at SOUASTRE
Water supply & troughs erected at COUIN
One section at IV Army Trench Mortar School designing & constructing trenchwork for emplacements &c

G. H. [illegible]
Major
R.E.

48

Army Form C. 2118.

Instructions regarding War Diaries and Intelligence Summaries are contained in F. S. Regs., Part II. and the Staff Manual respectively. Title pages will be prepared in manuscript.

WAR DIARY
~~or~~
~~INTELLIGENCE~~ ~~SUMMARY.~~

(Erase heading not required.) 1/2nd South Midland Field Co R.E.

Vol 14

39

Place	Date 1916 May	Hour	Summary of Events and Information	Remarks and references to Appendices
SOUASTRE	1		General work continued – No 4 section still at 4th Army Trench Mortar School VALHEUREUX	
	2		do	
	3		do No 4 Section moved to BEAUVAL – part employed at T M school & part on water supply scheme for BEAUVAL (under C E 8th Corps)	
	4		do	
	5		L & M Sections taken over by 46th Division All work at FONQUEVILLERS handed over to 2/1st North Midland Field Co R.E. Company except No 4 Section concentrated at ROSSIGNOL FARM for the night.	
HEM	6		Company marched to HEM	
	7		Company training commenced – programme of work comprises (1) pontoon & trestle (Weldon) bridging (2) knotting & lashing & use of spars (3) spar trestle bridging (4) catamaran barrel bridge (5) light suspension bridge (6) explosives & demolitions (7) route marching (8) engineer reconnaissance (9) semaphore signalling (10) close order drill (11) musketry – 30 yards range	
	8		Training continued	
	9		do	
	10		do	
	11		do	
	12		do	

1577 Wt. W10791/1773 500,000 1/15 D. D. & L. A.D.S.S./Forms/C. 2118.

Instructions regarding War Diaries and Intelligence Summaries are contained in F. S. Regs., Part II. and the Staff Manual respectively. Title pages will be prepared in manuscript.

WAR DIARY

~~or~~

~~INTELLIGENCE SUMMARY.~~

(Erase heading not required.) 1/2nd South Midland Field Co RE

Army Form C. 2118.

40

Place	Date 1916 May	Hour	Summary of Events and Information	Remarks and references to Appendices
HEM	13		General Training continued - No 4 section [illegible]	
	14		do	
	15		do - 1 NCO + 6 men attached T M School for construction work	
	16		do	
	17		do	
	18		do - Party of 6 detailed daily for [illegible] to Officers Casualty Clearing Station at GEZAINCOURT	
	19		do	
	20		do	
	21		do	
	22		do	
	23		do	
	24		do	
	25		do	
	26		do	
	27		do	
ROSSIGNOL FARM	28		Company marched to ROSSIGNOL FARM	
COIGNEUX	29		Officers + NCOs visit work at HEBUTERNE + RE Store ROSSIGNOL for taking over from 2/1 S M Field Co RE	
	30		Company took over from 2/1 S M Field Co RE 2 sections at HEBUTERNE - 2 sections at ROSSIGNOL	
	31		General work	

G. F. Eberle
Major
2 S M F Co RE

1577 Wt. W10791/1773 500,000 1/15 D. D. & L. A.D.S.S./Forms/C. 2118.

48

Army Form C. 2118.

Instructions regarding War Diaries and Intelligence Summaries are contained in F. S. Regs., Part II. and the Staff Manual respectively. Title pages will be prepared in manuscript.

WAR DIARY
or
~~INTELLIGENCE SUMMARY.~~

(*Erase heading not required.*) 1/2nd South Midland Field Co RE

41

Vol 15

Place	Date 1916 June	Hour	Summary of Events and Information	Remarks and references to Appendices
ROSSIGNOL FARM COIGNEUX	1		Work in hand	
			HEBUTERNE – Completion of 12 O.P.s – bulk of both sections employed on mining galleries & dugouts	
			Completion of new front & support trenches & communication in H sector	
			" " new support trench in G sector	
			General work for 143 Inf Brigade in G & H sectors	
			ROSSIGNOL – General work required by Division –	
			making mining frames & framed dugouts	
			one O.P. complete	
			huts for Divisional Staff	
			water troughs	
			Various special devices for concealing guns, aircraft signalling, collapsible huts etc	
			Water supply for horses at COUIN improved	
			New Baths at White bridge 500 yards W of SAILLY	
			New track across country from COUIN to COURCELLES	
			Hutting for ammunition supplies 400 yards S of BAYENCOURT	
			Maintenance of water supply at COIGNEUX & COUIN springs	
			General work in charge of 48th Divisional RE store	
	2		General work continued – Fire at Divisional RE store due to spontaneous combustion of stack of sandbags – 50000 sandbags 300 felt rolls } destroyed	
			Fire continued from 3 pm to 10 pm	
	3		do	
	4		do	
	5		do	

1577 Wt. W10791/1773 500,000 1/15 D. D. & L. A.D.S.S./Forms/C. 2118.

Instructions regarding War Diaries and Intelligence Summaries are contained in F. S. Regs., Part II. and the Staff Manual respectively. Title pages will be prepared in manuscript.

WAR DIARY
or
~~INTELLIGENCE SUMMARY.~~

(*Erase heading not required.*) 1/2nd South Midland Field Co R.E

Army Form C. 2118.

42

Place	1916 Date June	Hour	Summary of Events and Information	Remarks and references to Appendices
ROSSIGNOL FARM COIGNEUX	6		Work continues	
	7		ditto	
	8		ditto	
	9		ditto	
	10		ditto	
	11		ditto	
	12		ditto	
bivouac near SAILLY	13		Section at HEBUTERNE relieved by ~~other~~ 2 sections W of SAILLY – all horses & drivers remaining 2 sections & Company H.Q moved into bivouac 1000x W of SAILLY – work at RE Store handed over to 2/1st S M Field Co at ROSSIGNOL – work at RE Store handed over to 2/1st S M Field Co 2 sections at SAILLY employed on OP's & record dugouts for same in old French Trench 100x W of PATIN	
	14		do	
	15		do	
	16		do	
	17		do	
	18		do	
	19		do	
	20		do	
	21		do	
	22		do 1½ sections withdrawn from HEBUTERNE, leaving 1 officer & 19 O.R. for store, watersupply & general RE work. Work on OP's completed – Antigas blankets erected in all OP's, battalion & company H.Q & signal offices – Heavy rain during night	
	23		bombardment of enemy's trenches commenced 6.0 am.	
	24		Sections at SAILLY rested – HEBUTERNE unaltered – bombardment continues	
	25		New route from SAILLY ~~to~~ HEBUTERNE commenced – bombardment continued	
	26		work on new route	

Instructions regarding War Diaries and Intelligence Summaries are contained in F. S. Regs., Part II. and the Staff Manual respectively. Title pages will be prepared in manuscript.

WAR DIARY
or
~~INTELLIGENCE SUMMARY.~~
(Erase heading not required.) 1/2nd South Midland Field Co. RE.

Army Form C. 2118.

43

Place	Date June	Hour	Summary of Events and Information	Remarks and references to Appendices
Bivouac near SAILLY	27		New route from SAILLY to HEBUTERNE completed & marked by posts - [illegible] bridges over trenches	
			Bombardment continued - heavy rain during night 27/28	
	28		do - section in front line employed on [illegible] water supply in trenches by 2-600 gallon tanks to water supply at junctions of JENA & AUERSTADT with VERCINGETORIX, also repair of heavy T. M. emplacement - attack postponed 24 hours	
	29		do. During night of 29/30 two dummy trenches 50 yards apart marked out & dug in 2 hours by 400 men - total length 1320 yards. Orders received at 10.30 & working party commenced at 12.40 am (at bivouac)	
	30		do. Sections prepared for the attack, packing up, sharpening bayonets etc. Pumps at COLIN & COLGNOUX taken over from 2nd Anglesey RE	
			G. F. Eberle [illegible] Major 2 S M Fd Co RE	

1577 Wt. W10791/1773 500,000 1/15 D. D. & L. A.D.S.S./Forms/C. 2118.

Instructions regarding War Diaries and Intelligence Summaries are contained in F. S. Regs., Part II. and the Staff Manual respectively. Title pages will be prepared in manuscript.

WAR DIARY
or
~~INTELLIGENCE SUMMARY.~~

(Erase heading not required.) 1/2nd South Midland Field Co RE

Army Form C. 2118.

Vol 16

Place	Date	Hour	Summary of Events and Information	Remarks and references to Appendices
Bivouac near Sailly	1916 July 1		VIII Corps attacked on right of 143 Inf. Brigade & 56th Divn on left – 143 Inf Brigade did not attack & company remained at bivouac all day	
	2		Remained in bivouac	
	3		do – relieved Officer & 20 men at HEBUTERNE – this party had heavy work throughout the bombardment owing to heavy German shelling of trenches & village – repairing T.M. emplacements, broken water pipes etc	
	4		do – 144 Inf Brigade relieved 31st Divn in COLINCAMPS Sector	
Rossignol	5		Moved to ROSSIGNOL – 145 Inf Brigade relieved 143 Inf. Brigade & 1st Field Co relieved detachment at HEBUTERNE. Took over RE store COIGNEUX & all pumping stations & work in back area	
	6		general work – heavy rain	
	7		do – 2 sections sent to COURCELLES to work under 3/1 S Mid Fd Co in the COLINCAMPS Sector, repairing trenches – very heavy rain all day	
	8		do	
	9		do	
	10		do	
	11		do	
	12		do	
	13		do – orders received for move tomorrow & to handover store & billets to 1/1 S M Fd Co	
ALBERT	14		Company moved to ALBERT & placed under orders of C E X Corps	
	15		All sappers employed on repair of main road ALBERT – BAPAUME from original German ~~British~~ front trench to X 8 d 7·0	Map 57D SE
	16		48 Divn having arrived the company again came under orders of C.R.E. Parties from each section reconnoitred the area OVILLERS to ALBERT – BAPAUME road & the trenches adjoining road on SE side.	

1577 Wt. W10791/1773 500,000 1/15 D. D. & L. A.D.S.S./Forms/C. 2118.

Instructions regarding War Diaries and Intelligence Summaries are contained in F. S. Regs., Part II. and the Staff Manual respectively. Title pages will be prepared in manuscript.

WAR DIARY
or
~~INTELLIGENCE~~ SUMMARY.
(Erase heading not required.) 1/2nd South Midland Field Co RE

Army Form C. 2118.

45

Place	Date July	Hour	Summary of Events and Information	Remarks and references to Appendices
ALBERT			32nd & 25 Divisions relieved by 48th Divn	
			2 pumps in ALBERT taken over	
			reconnaissance of water supply at LA BOISSELLE	
			1 section at work on communication trench to OVILLERS	
	17		1 section placed at disposal of 145 Inf Brigade for operations NE of OVILLERS – this section was not used	
			2 sections employed with 106th & 130th Field Companies on improving communications in OVILLERS sector	
	18		1 section attached to infantry for front line work & quartered in German dugout at X 8 b 75. At 2 30pm this section assisted in bombing attack by 6th Warwicks, by carrying up bombs under heavy fire	
			1 section employed at night with 2 Companies 5/Sussex pioneers on digging trench from X 2d 44 to X 3 c 0.2 & deepening trench from X 3 c 0.2 to X 3 c 93	Map 57 D SE Edition 2B
			1 officer (Lieut Perry) & party assisted 1/ Sussex Co in laying out new trenches about X 3d – X 9b	
			Reconnaisance by 1 officer (Lieut Perry) of wood at X 4 c 5 2 which he found to be held by us	
			Casualties 1 O.R wounded	
	19		3 sections with 2 Companies 5/Sussex pioneers employed by night on trenches X 2d 44 & 83, X 3 c 02 & 93 & construction of strong points at first three and X 8 b 78	
			Section in the line engaged on general repair to trenches & to well in SE corner of OVILLERS	
			2 officers (Lieut Perry & Watts) & 8 O.R. wounded (1 off & 4 OR slightly); 1 O R killed	

1577 Wt. W10791/1773 500,000 1/15 D. D. & L. A.D.S.S./Forms/C. 2118.

WAR DIARY

or

~~INTELLIGENCE SUMMARY.~~

(*Erase heading not required.*) 1/2nd South Midland Field Co RE

Army Form C. 2118.

46

Instructions regarding War Diaries and Intelligence Summaries are contained in F. S. Regs., Part II. and the Staff Manual respectively. Title pages will be prepared in manuscript.

Place	Date 1916	Hour	Summary of Events and Information	Remarks and references to Appendices
ALBERT	July 20		Headquarters & 3 sections moved into bivouacs on road between ALBERT & AVELUY. Reconnaissance for OPs on ALBERT – BAPAUME road & TARA HILL – two suitable OPs found & repaired	
	21		Sections in front line relieved. One section engaged on making up track W17c 6-7 to W23a 5-9½ & flooded area. Horselines moved to BOUZINCOURT. casualties – 1 O.R. wounded	
	22		One further section attached to 145 Inf Brigade for night operations. Sections not used but 1 Officer (Lieut Watts) laid out tape 450x as forming up line for night attacking battalion (4 Oxford & Bucks). Attack successful & objectives gained viz X3c79, X3d 28 & 97. Section on right quartered in LA BOISSELLE. Section employed with 1/1 S Mid Fd Co on digging communication trench LA BOISSELLE	
	23		Section employed on ... LA BOISSELLE from X3d03 to 28. 1 further section employed on cleaning out trench from X8b [illegible] to X3c0-2 but it was found having been sent up to make strong point at X3c39 that we had lost possession. casualties – 1 O.R. wounded. Sections in front of OVILLERS & at LA BOISSELLE withdrawn in the morning being relieved by 1/1 S Mid Fd Co	
BOUZINCOURT	24	6 pm	All sappers moved to Bivouacs near wagon lines at BOUZINCOURT. 1 section at Divl RE Store, work on baths & repair of buildings	
	25		3 sections employed on strong points at OVILLERS, digging trenches & fire recesses & wiring. Division to be relieved by 12th Division – 70th Field Co RE took over	
LEALVILLERS	26		Company marched to LEALVILLERS & bivouaced	
	27		Company rested – placed under orders of 145 Infantry Brigade	

1577 Wt. W10791/1773 500,000 1/15 D. D. & L. A.D.S.S./Forms/C. 2118.

Army Form C. 2118.

Instructions regarding War Diaries and Intelligence Summaries are contained in F. S. Regs., Part II. and the Staff Manual respectively. Title pages will be prepared in manuscript.

WAR DIARY
or
~~INTELLIGENCE SUMMARY.~~

(Erase heading not required.) 1/2nd South Midland Field Co. R.E.

47

Place	Date	Hour	Summary of Events and Information	Remarks and references to Appendices
	1916 July			
BEAUVAL	28		Company marched with 145 Inf Brigade to BEAUVAL & went into billets for the night	
CRAMONT	29		March resumed – Company went into billets at LE MENAGE near CRAMONT after a long & trying march in hot sun (15 miles) – 12 men fell out	
	30		Company rested	
	31		Light work – general overhaul, drill & musketry instruction	

G. F. Eberle maj
1/2nd S M Field Co. R.E.

1577 Wt. W10791/1773 500,000 1/15 D. D. & L. A.D.S.S./Forms/C. 2118.

48th Divisional Engineers

1/2nd SOUTH MIDLAND FIELD COMPANY R. E.

AUGUST 1 9 1 6

Army Form C. 2118.

Instructions regarding War Diaries and Intelligence Summaries are contained in F. S. Regs., Part II. and the Staff Manual respectively. Title pages will be prepared in manuscript.

WAR DIARY or ~~INTELLIGENCE SUMMARY.~~

(Erase heading not required.) 1/2nd South Midland Field Co RE.

48

Place	Date 1916 August	Hour	Summary of Events and Information	Remarks and references to Appendices
CRAMONT	1		Company resting - light work only - drill & musketry instruction. Erected shower baths for 145 Inf. Brigade & water troughs for several villages	
	2		do	
	3		Sappers with bridging wagons marched to l'Etoile & bivouached at CAESAR'S CAMP	
	4		Pontoon practice on the SOMME	
	5		do - sappers returned to CRAMONT in the evening - 2/Lt Henderson (Kent RE) joined	
	6		Company rested - 2/Lts Hull, Sharp, Wright & Knight (Kent RE) joined	
	7		Light work only	
LONGVILLERS	8		Lt Barrett (Kent RE) joined - Company marched to LONGVILLERS & bivouached	
AUTHIEULE	9		Company marched to AUTHIEULE & bivouached	
ACHEUX	10		" " " ACHEUX & billeted there	
	11		rested	
	12		do	
AVELUY	13		Company marched to AVELUY & bivouached - wagons & horses at BOUZINCOURT. Took over sector north of OVILLERS with frontage X2c37 to X2d47	57D SE(4) OVILLERS 1/10000 Ed. 2B
	14		2 sections moved into forward dugouts at DONNET POST (W12D83) & employed on construction of strong points & deepening & repairing communication trenches, which had been badly blown in. All four sections engaged (by night) in the work	
	15		do. One section attached to 144 Inf. Brigade for operation but was not called on & was employed on deepening a communication trench.	
	16		Forward sections relieved - all four sections worked on forward strong points & communication trenches	
	17		2 sections on forward work - 2 sections on mining dugout for machine gun crews in OVILLERS & completing emplacements - Casualties 1 Officer 6 OR wounded. New trenches at X1D79 - X1B90 & X1B52 to X2C26 reconnoitred	

1577 Wt. W10791/1773 500,000 1/15 D. D. & L. A.D.S.S./Forms/C. 2118.

Instructions regarding War Diaries and Intelligence Summaries are contained in F. S. Regs., Part II. and the Staff Manual respectively. Title pages will be prepared in manuscript.

or

INTELLIGENCE SUMMARY.

(Erase heading not required.) 1/2nd South Midland Field Co RE.

49

Place	Date 1916 Augt	Hour	Summary of Events and Information	Remarks and references to Appendices
AVELUY	18		Company attached to 143 Inf Brigade for operation Front trenches reconnoitred by OC & [illegible] in the morning 1st objective – X2b62 – 20 – 03 X2a 91 – 81 X2c 39 2nd " X2b33 – 44 – 06 X2a 96 – 76 – 56 – 43 – 22 3rd X2b59 78 48 1 Forward RE officer & 6 Sappers attached to each of the assaulting battalions 5th & 6th battalion R Warwick Regt Remainder of 2 section ordered to OVILLERS. Attack commenced 8.5 pm & all objectives gained by about 8.0 pm – infantry holdup sometime at X2b62 Over 400 prisoners & 9 officers captured Left RE section ordered to move up at 7.35 pm by Forward Officer Right 8.30 pm by OC as news being received from FO Left section reopened communication between X2b90 – 62 – 44 & consolidated strong point at 62. Right section assisted in repelling enemy counterattack about 8.30 pm & cleared communication between X2c88 & X2a81 Two sections relieved about at 3.0 am & consolidated points in first & second objectives	
	19		One section consolidated trench X2a 96 – 76 working within 50 yards of the enemy	
	20		Two sections rested – 2 sections employed on clearing up – front X1B13 to X2a22 taken over from 49th Division	
	21		Two sections attached to 144 Inf Brigade for attack on trench X1B18 to R31D818 X2a19 – Second objective X1B19 ~~R31C…~~ to R31D64 – 83 Attack launched 6.0 pm & first objective gained, also nearly all second objective but not point 62 – 83 7th Brigade 25th Division which had relieved 49th Division assisted by simultaneous attack on our left.	

1577 Wt. W10791/1773 500,000 1/15 D. D. & L. A.D.S.S./Forms/C. 2118.

Instructions regarding War Diaries and Intelligence Summaries are contained in F. S. Regs., Part II. and the Staff Manual respectively. Title pages will be prepared in manuscript.

or

INTELLIGENCE SUMMARY.

(*Erase heading not required.*) 1/2nd South Midland Field Co. R.E.

50

Place	Date 1916 Aug	Hour	Summary of Events and Information	Remarks and references to Appendices
AVELUY	21 cont		One section attached to 4th Battn Glo. Regt:- new communication trench from old British line X1B 03½ to 18 reconnoitred & marked out with tapes (250 yards). Working party of 200 infantry under RE supervision dug this to depth of 4' before dawn. New communication trench from X1C 99½ to X2a 22 marked out. Working party of 100 infantry under RE supervision dug this to average depth of 3' before dawn. Section RE consolidated captured trench at X1B 19	
			One section attached to 1/6th Battn Glos Regt - was unable to work beyond X2a 19 owing to hostile bombing attacks from R 32c 31 & so reopened communication between X2a 16 & 19	
			About 4 officers & 150 prisoners taken in this attack.	
	22		Two sections with infantry working parties continued work of preceding night.	
	23		One section attached to 144 Inf Brigade for small attack on X2a 79: attack failed & section not called on, so employed in clearing trench X2a 25-46 & improving forward trenches generally	
			One section & infantry working parties employed on X1D 69-22	
	24		One section worked on forward trenches X2a 25-46-27-29 & towards 79. All these trenches had been badly blown in by enemy shelling. Work stopped at 3.30 am owing to heavy shellfire X2c 88-X2a 80 & northwards X2b 20-96	
			One section with 100 carrying party formed forward RE dumps at X2a 22 & X8a 03 Working party of 40 improved C.T. X1a 96-X1B 09-X2a 22	

1577 Wt. W10791/1773 500,000 1/15 D. D. & L. A.D.S.S./Forms/C. 2118.

Army Form C. 2118.

Instructions regarding War Diaries and Intelligence Summaries are contained in F. S. Regs., Part II. and the Staff Manual respectively. Title pages will be prepared in manuscript.

or

INTELLIGENCE SUMMARY.

(*Erase heading not required.*) 1/2nd South Midland Field Co RE — 51

Place	Date 1916 Aug	Hour	Summary of Events and Information	Remarks and references to Appendices
AVELUY	25		All sections very much exhausted & given a night's rest	
	26		2 sections with infantry working parties employed in clearing out & reopening forward communication trenches & support line X 2 a 39-80-81 - X 2 B 03-20-62	
	27		Company relieved by 105 Field Co RE (25th Division) & marched to BOUZINCOURT	
	28		Marched to AUTHIE & went into billets	
	29		Rested	
	30		Light work - squad drill, physical drill & rifle instruction	
	31		do	

G. F. [illegible] Major RE
Comd 1/2nd S.M. Field Co RE

1577 Wt. W10791/1773 500,000 1/15 D. D. & L. A.D.S.S./Forms/C. 2118.

1/2nd. S. M. FIELD COY. ROYAL ENGINEERS

S E P T E M B E R 1 9 1 6.

Vol 18

Confidential

War Diary

of

1/2nd S M Field Co RE 48th Div

From 1st September 1916 to 30th September 1916

Vol 19

C O N F I D E N T I A L .

W A R   D I A R Y

o f

1/2nd (South Midland) Field Company, R.E.

48th Division.

From 1st October 1916 ....to...........31st October 1916.

Instructions regarding War Diaries and Intelligence Summaries are contained in F. S. Regs., Part II. and the Staff Manual respectively. Title pages will be prepared in manuscript.

WAR DIARY
or
~~INTELLIGENCE~~ SUMMARY.

(*Erase heading not required.*) 1/2nd South Midland Field Co RE

Army Form C. 2118.

52

Place	Date	Hour	Summary of Events and Information	Remarks and references to Appendices
AUTHIE	1916 Sept 1		Company training – squad drill, physical drill, musketry instruction, bayonet training	
	2		do	
	3		do	
	4		do	
	5		Route march – NCOs lectures & map reading – use of compass by night	
	6		Company training	
	7		Route march – NCOs surveying instruction	
	8		Company training	
	9		do – reconnaissance of trenches in AUCHONVILLERS sector with a view to taking over from 2/1 S Mid Field Co	
	10		Rested	
HEM	11		Marched to HEM	
	12		Company training resumed including pontooning	
	13		do – water supply reconnaissance in the area	
	14		do do	
	15		do billet survey of BEAUVAL for winter accommodation	
	16		do	
	17		do	
OUTREBOIS	18		Marched to OUTREBOIS	
	19		Company training resumed, including demolition, boring & levelling & surveying	
	20		do	

1577 Wt. W10791/1773 500,000 1/15 D. D. & L. A.D.S.S./Forms/C. 2118.

Instructions regarding War Diaries and Intelligence Summaries are contained in F. S. Regs., Part II. and the Staff Manual respectively. Title pages will be prepared in manuscript.

WAR DIARY
or
~~INTELLIGENCE SUMMARY.~~

(Erase heading not required.) 1/2nd South Midland Field Co RE

Army Form C. 2118.

58

Place	Date 1916 Sept.	Hour	Summary of Events and Information	Remarks and references to Appendices
OUTREBOIS	21		Company training continues	
	22		do	
	23		do - one section took part in field operation with 5 R War R	
BERNAVILLE	24		Marched to BERNAVILLE	
	25		Company training	
	26		Company entrenchment & field operation with 143 Inf Brigade	
	27		Company training including Semaphore signalling & extended order work	
	28		do	
CAUMESNIL	29		Marched to CAUMESNIL near ORVILLE	
	30		Rested	

[illegible] Major
2 S Mid RE

Instructions regarding War Diaries and Intelligence Summaries are contained in F. S. Regs., Part II. and the Staff Manual respectively. Title pages will be prepared in manuscript.

WAR DIARY
or
~~INTELLIGENCE SUMMARY.~~

(Erase heading not required.) 1/2nd South Midland Field Co RE

Army Form C. 2118.

54

Place	Date	Hour	Summary of Events and Information	Remarks and references to Appendices
	1916 Octr			
COUIN/ETNIL	1		Rested	
	2		Marched to SAILLY (HQ & 1 Section) & HEBUTERNE (3 sections) & relieved 212th Field Co (33rd Division) in sector between HEBUTERNE - PUISIEUX road & GOMMECOURT wood	
	3		continued construction of deep dugouts & cleaning & revetting front trenches	
HENU	4		relieved by 1/1st [illegible] Field Co. & 77th Field Co (17 Divn) & marched to HENU	
	5		Hutting - conversion of stables into hutments for a battalion	
	6		do do - erection of ammunition dump on HENU - St AMAND road	
	7		do do (completed) do	
	8		- erection of meat shed for Divl Train at WARLINCOURT	
	9		do - commenced hutting for 1 battalion at SOUASTRE do do (completed)	
	10		do	
	11		do	
	12		do	
	13		do SOUASTRE camp completed	
	14		do commenced hutting for 1 battalion at HENU	
	15		do	
	16		do	
	17		do	
	18		do HENU hutting completed	
	19		do erection of stables for Divl HQ	
	20		do	
WARLINCOURT	21		Company marched to WARLINCOURT	

1577 Wt. W10791/1773 500,000 1/15 D. D. & L. A.D.S.S./Forms/C. 2118.

Instructions regarding War Diaries and Intelligence Summaries are contained in F. S. Regs., Part II. and the Staff Manual respectively. Title pages will be prepared in manuscript.

WAR DIARY
or
~~INTELLIGENCE SUMMARY.~~

Army Form C. 2118.

(Erase heading not required.) 1/2nd South Midland Field Co RE 55

Place	Date	Hour	Summary of Events and Information	Remarks and references to Appendices
	1916 Oct			
WARLINCOURT	22		Rested	
	23		do	
	24		All horses & wagons marched in a convoy to TALMAS	
FRANVILLERS	25		Sappers moved by motor bus to FRANVILLERS	
			Transport marched to do.	
MAMETZ WOOD	26		Marched to MAMETZ WOOD & bivouaced in tents & shelters - several wagons bogged & left for the night 500 yards from the camp	
			Transport parked near CONTALMAISON	
	27		Company employed on repair of old German Road (MAMETZ to BAZENTIN) S 14 B 0-6 to X 24 C 5-1 - with 6th R War Regt	
	28		do	
	29		do	
	30		do	
	31		do	

G F Herb[illegible] Major

2nd S Mid Field Co RE.

1577 Wt. W10791/1773 500,000 1/15 D. D. & L. A.D.S.S./Forms/C. 2118.

Vol 20

Confidential

War Diary

of

1/2nd South Midland Field Co. R.E.

48th Division

From 1st November 1916 - to - 30th November 1916

(Ops. 56-57.)

Instructions regarding War Diaries and Intelligence Summaries are contained in F. S. Regs., Part II. and the Staff Manual respectively. Title pages will be prepared in manuscript.

WAR DIARY
or
~~INTELLIGENCE SUMMARY.~~
(Erase heading not required.) 1/2nd South Midland Field Co. RE

Army Form C. 2118.

56

Place	Date 1916	Hour	Summary of Events and Information	Remarks and references to Appendices
MAMETZ WOOD	Novemb 1		Work continued on old German road – 48 Div began relief of 15 Div. – the company in reserve	
	2		do	
	3		do – 1 section sent to MARTINPUICH for work on M G positions under 3 Bgde	
	4		HQ & 3 sections moved to dugouts in SHELTER WOOD VALLEY (X22C91) exchanging with 73rd Field Co (15 Div.) Wagon line moved to LA BOISSELLE	
SHELTER WOOD VALLEY	5		Work on road CONTALMAISON to CONTALMAISON VILLA Work on road CONTALMAISON & started new Divisional store 1 section took over RE store CONTALMAISON at X16B25	
	6		do – 120' siding a new store commenced	
	7		do – hutting (new office & messes) at Divisional Headquarters commenced road handed over to 91st Field Co.	
	8		do	
	9		do	
	10		do	
	11		do	
	12		do	
	13		do	
	14		do	
	15		do – Section at MARTINPUICH relieved	
	16		do	
	17		do	
	18		do	
	19		do	
	20		do	

1577 Wt. W10791/1773 500,000 1/15 D. D. & L. A.D.S.S./Forms/C. 2118.

Instructions regarding War Diaries and Intelligence Summaries are contained in F. S. Regs., Part II. and the Staff Manual respectively. Title pages will be prepared in manuscript.

WAR DIARY
or
INTELLIGENCE SUMMARY.

(Erase heading not required.) 1/2nd South Midland Field Co R E.

Army Form C. 2118.

57

Place	Date 1916	Hour	Summary of Events and Information	Remarks and references to Appendices
SHELTER WOOD VALLEY	Nov. 21		General work continued – Platform, tramway siding & road diversion at VILLA STATION (X 11 C 32) commenced	
	22		do 240' cutting for garage at D HQ commenced	
	23		do	
	24		do	
	25		do – section at MARTINPUICH relieved	
	26		do	
	27		do	
			do – setting & laying out Dvl RA wagon lines	
	28		do	
	29		do	
	30		Summary	
			Hutting at D H Q – New huts erected for G.O.C.'s mess, A & Q Office, G clerk office, CRE office & mess, RA office	
			Cookhouse, fittings & general work	
			Platform & road at CONTALMAISON VILLA completed	
			New RE store completed with 120' x 25' road siding & platform, store house & tramway siding 200 ft long	
			Garage at D H Q practically completed	
			G. F. Ebel[?] Major 1/2 S M Fd Co RE	

1577 Wt. W10791/1773 500,000 1/15 D. D. & L. A.D.S.S./Forms/C. 2118.

Vol 21

C O N F I D E N T I A L

W A R   D I A R Y

of

1/2nd (S.M.) F I E L D   C O M P A N Y R.E.

From 1st December 1916.....to.....31st December 1916.

Vols. 58 to 59.

Army Form C. 2118.

WAR DIARY
or
~~INTELLIGENCE SUMMARY.~~

Instructions regarding War Diaries and Intelligence Summaries are contained in F. S. Regs., Part II. and the Staff Manual respectively. Title pages will be prepared in manuscript.

(*Erase heading not required.*) 1/2nd SOUTH MIDLAND FIELD Co RE

58

Place	Date 1916	Hour	Summary of Events and Information	Remarks and references to Appendices
SHELTER WOOD VALLEY	Dec 1		General work continued – Hutting at DHQ – motor garage & siding RA mess hut & sleeping accommodation Commanders Incinerator & drying room One section at MARTINPUICH for work on Corps intermediate line Work at RE dump – making oil drum stoves erecting sawmill engine & shed general running of store	
	2		do	
	3		do	
	4		do	
	5		do – section at MARTINPUICH relieved – garage completed	
	6		do	
	7		do	
	8		do – RA mess completed	
	9		do	
	10		do	
	11		do	
	12		do incinerator & drying room completed	
	13		do	
	14		do – section at MARTINPUICH relieved by 91st & 74th Field Co	
BAZENTIN LE PETIT	15		48 Divn relieved by 15th Divn & company came under CRE 15 Divn Billets exchanged with 1/1 [illegible] Field Co & company moved to north of MAMETZ WOOD (S 14 B 15)	

1577 Wt. W10791/1773 500,000 1/15 D. D. & L. A.D.S.S./Forms/C. 2118.

Army Form C. 2118.

WAR DIARY
or
INTELLIGENCE SUMMARY.

Instructions regarding War Diaries and Intelligence Summaries are contained in F. S. Regs., Part II. and the Staff Manual respectively. Title pages will be prepared in manuscript.

(*Erase heading not required.*) 1/2nd SOUTH MIDLAND FIELD Co RE 59

Place	Date	Hour	Summary of Events and Information	Remarks and references to Appendices
BAZENTIN LE PETIT	1916 Dec 16		Company employed on new tramline X17A93 to X17C30 completion of water point at X17C30 maintenance of VILLAWOOD tramline West of BAZENTIN LE PETIT WOOD work at 48th Div. Bomb store work on camp improvement at S14B15 1 section moved to W29B for erection of NISSEN HUTS & horselines for Div. Train Camp	
	17		do	
	18		do – 10 men sent to LAVIEVILLE for erection of huts for D.A.C	
	19		do	
	20		do – 1 section moved to MILLENCOURT for construction of infantry camp	
	21		do – 1 section commenced enlargement of camp at X19D29	
	22		do	
	23		do – work on new tramline handed over to 1/1 South Mid Fd Co	
	24		do – working party of 200 on CHAPEISAUR road	
	25		general holiday	
	26		work continued	
	27		do	
	28		do	
	29		do	
	30		do – Maj G.F. EBERLE becomes acting CRE 48th Div in absence of CRE	
	31		do	

[signature] Major RE

1577 Wt. W10791/1773 500,000 1/15 D. D. & L. A.D.S.S./Forms/C. 2118.

Vol 22

C O N F I D E N T I A L.

W A R D I A R Y

of

1/2nd. (South Midland) Field Company, R.E.

from 1st January 1917........to..........31st January 1917.

Army Form C. 2118.

Instructions regarding War Diaries and Intelligence Summaries are contained in F. S. Regs., Part II. and the Staff Manual respectively. Title pages will be prepared in manuscript.

WAR DIARY
or
~~INTELLIGENCE SUMMARY.~~

(Erase heading not required.)

1/2nd S. Mid. Field Coy R.E.

60

Place	Date 1917	Hour	Summary of Events and Information	Remarks and references to Appendices
BAZENTIN LE PETIT	Jan 1st		The Company took over the following works from 1/1 S. M. Field Coy R.E. Tramway to CONTALMAISON Camps in X17 Water Supply do at X23a 38. Erection of huts & dugout at Div. Gas School – X21d " Y.M.C.A. huts at BECOURT & SCOTS REDOUBT X21b " Nissen Huts for R.A. at X22a & LA BOISSELLE X19b Repair of hut at CONTALMAISON CHATEAU. Work on Camps in 15th Div. Area	
	2nd		Above works continued & Tramway from LA BOISSELLE to CHAPES SPUR reconnoitred & reported on.	
	3		Do. Supervision of R.A. O.P's handed over to 73rd Field Coy R.E. Y.M.C.A. hut at SCOTS REDOUBT X21b handed over to 1/1 S. M. Field Coy Rifle Range at MILLENCOURT completed & handed over to 2nd of Bde.	
	4		Do. 1 Section returned from MILLENCOURT to Coy Hd Qrs less eleven men detached to BECOURT for work on YMCA hut. R.A. Nissen Huts at LA BOISSELLE completed.	
	5		Do. 1 Section return from Divl Train Camp & detachment of 11 from BECOURT to Coy Hd Qrs. 2 Sections come under orders of C.E. III Corps for wiring Corps Line. Details taken over from 50th Div. R.E. & work started.	
	6		Do. LA BOISSELLE – CHAPES SPUR Tramway – Work on Gas School, Camps & Y.M.C.A. hut at BECOURT handed over to 1/1 S. M. Field Coy Tramway to CONTALMAISON CAMPS (X17) & Water Supply (X23a 38) completed.	

1577 Wt. W10791/1773 500,000 1/15 D. D. & L. A.D.S.S./Forms/C. 2118.

Instructions regarding War Diaries and Intelligence Summaries are contained in F. S. Regs., Part II. and the Staff Manual respectively. Title pages will be prepared in manuscript.

WAR DIARY
or
~~INTELLIGENCE SUMMARY.~~
(Erase heading not required.)

1/2 S. Mid Field Coy R.E

Army Form C. 2118.

61

Place	Date Jan 17	Hour	Summary of Events and Information	Remarks and references to Appendices
BAZENTIN LE PETIT	7th		2 Secs carry on with wiring on Corps 2nd Line.	
	8		The whole Coy come under C.E III Corps for work on wiring ~~2nd~~ Corps 2nd Line.	
	9		Wiring Corps 2nd Line continued.	
	10		"	
	11		"	
	12		"	
	13		"	
	14		"	
	15		"	
	16		"	
	17		"	
	18		"	
	19		"	
	20		"	
	21		"	
	22		"	
	23		"	
	24		"	
	25		"	
	26		"	
	27	8.40 a.m.	Company move to MERICOURT - SUR - SOMME via FRICOURT, MEAULTE, MORLANCOURT. completed by 2.30 pm	
	28		Coy Resting	
	29		Coy parades for drill etc & lecture.	
	30		Do	
	31	1 pm	Coy move to FRISE via BRAY, SUZANNE. R.E. Store near HERBECOURT G30a taken over. Reconnaissance made of dispositions held by 2/7 Coy 3rd Regt de Génie preparatory to relieving them on following day.	

W Ebele Capt
1/2 S. Mid Field Coy RE.

1577 Wt. W10791/1773 500,000 1/15 D. D. & L. A.D.S.S./Forms/C. 2118.

Vol 23

War Diary of

475th (S.M.) Field Company R.E.

for month of

February 1917.

Pps 40

Instructions regarding War Diaries and Intelligence Summaries are contained in F. S. Regs., Part II. and the Staff Manual respectively. Title pages will be prepared in manuscript.

WAR DIARY
or
~~INTELLIGENCE SUMMARY.~~
(*Erase heading not required.*)

475 (S. Mid) Field Coy R.E.

62.

Army Form C. 2118.

Place	Date Feb /17	Hour	Summary of Events and Information	Remarks and references to Appendices
FRISE	1		Reconnaissance of Sector of Front Line on which the 2/7 Coy, 3rd Regt du Génie were employed made by small parties	Map 62 c N.W. 1/20,000
		6:30pm	Two Sections of the Coy (Nos 3 & 4) take over the dispositions of 2/7 Coy (French), including forward area billets & stores. These dugouts situated at H [illegible] 29 b 52 HdQrs & 2 Sections remain in Dugouts at G 16 d 85.	
	2		General Work & Reconnaissance.	
	3		do	
	4		do	
	5		HdQrs move to new dugouts at G 24 b 83	
	6		Reconnaissance of III Corps Line & sitting of M.G. positions areas(?). O.P. for 143rd Bde (Inf) started. 2 O.P.s for Divisional RA. General front line work, including overland wires, Revetting, etc. Divisional R.E. Store at G 30 a 40 taken over from French on their evacuation.	
	7		General Work as above	
	8		do	
	9		Two back Sections (Nos 1 & 2) relieve Forward Sections. Latter take over fresh dugouts from French at G 24 b 64.	
	10		General Work continued as above	
	11		do	
	12		do	
	13		do	
	14		do { Tunnelled M.G. position in front line N of BIACHES started	
	15		do	
	16		do	
	17		do Nos 3 & 4 Sections relieve front Sections	
	18		do	
	19		do	
	20		do Work on Trench Mortar Emplacements started	

1577 Wt. W10791/1773 500,000 1/15 D. D. & L. A.D.S.S./Forms/C. 2118.

Instructions regarding War Diaries and Intelligence Summaries are contained in F. S. Regs., Part II. and the Staff Manual respectively. Title pages will be prepared in manuscript.

WAR DIARY
or
~~INTELLIGENCE SUMMARY.~~

(*Erase heading not required.*)

475 (S.M.) Field Coy R.E.

Army Form C. 2118.

63.

Place	Date Feb/17	Hour	Summary of Events and Information	Remarks and references to Appendices
FRISE	21		General Front Line Work Continued. Construction of Inf & R.A. O.P's – Trench Mortar Emplacements – M.G. tunnelled Positions – Revetment of Trenches – Strengthening & increasing accommodation in dug outs. Repair of Roads in left forward area & trench board tracks laid, etc.	
	22		Do	
	23		Do	
	24		Do	
	25		Do. Nos 1 & 2 Secs relieve forward Sections	
	26		Do	
	27		Do	
	28		Do.	

[illegible] Capt.
O.C. 475 (S.M.) Field Coy
R.E.

A5834 Wt. W4973/M687 750,000 8/16 D. D. & L. Ltd. Forms/C.2118/13.

Vol 24

War Diary

of 475th (S.M.) Field Company R.E.

for

Month of

March 1917 — pps 64 to 67.

Instructions regarding War Diaries and Intelligence Summaries are contained in F. S. Regs., Part II. and the Staff Manual respectively. Title pages will be prepared in manuscript.

WAR DIARY
or
~~INTELLIGENCE SUMMARY.~~

(Erase heading not required.)

Army Form C. 2118.

475 (SOUTH MIDLAND) FIELD CO RE

64

Place	Date 1917	Hour	Summary of Events and Information	Remarks and references to Appendices
FRISE	March 1		General front line work - Construction of OPs - T.M. emplacements - Dugouts - Regt. Aid Post, Trench board track - maintenance of road & general upkeep of front line system. Wiring Corps line & intermediate line	
	2		do	
	3		do	
	4		do	
	5		do Section relieved	
	6		do	
	7		do	
	8		do	
	9		do	
	10		do	
	11		do Many fires seen in PERONNE & other places, indicating probable withdrawal by the enemy	
	12		do	
	13		do Section relieved	
	14		do	
	15		do	
		11 P.M	Information received that enemy probably about to retire. Orders to prepare for crossing canal (infantry footbridge to be followed by medium bridge) at BAZINCOURT FARM. Two pontoon wagons taken to BUSCOURT Lock, pontoon placed in water out of observation & superstructure concealed - canal crossing reconnoitred at site of old bridge which blocked canal	
	16		One trestle wagon & remaining 4 pontoon wagons of Divl. RE taken up in the evening - pontoons launched at BUSCOURT Lock & towed to SORMONT FARM - superstructure taken to SORMONT FARM together with a trestle of 9 x 3 for centre of canal (18' legs). Raft formed at SORMONT FARM & superstructure moved up to BAZINCOURT FARM. Great difficulties encountered, many snags, 9 trees lying across canal & under water, which had to be sawn through & cleared & 200 yards of ice 1-1½" thick	

A5834 Wt. W4973/M687 750,000 8/16 D. D. & L. Ltd. Forms/C.2118/13.

Instructions regarding War Diaries and Intelligence Summaries are contained in F. S. Regs., Part II. and the Staff Manual respectively. Title pages will be prepared in manuscript.

WAR DIARY
or
~~INTELLIGENCE SUMMARY.~~

(*Erase heading not required.*) 475 (SOUTH MIDLAND) FIELD Co R E

Army Form C. 2118.

65

Place	Date	Hour	Summary of Events and Information	Remarks and references to Appendices
FRISE	1917 March 16		First raft took 4 hours to reach site of bridge, altho' distance from LORMONT FARM is less than 1 mile – further difficulties due to a very dark night & to the necessity of avoiding noise; the enemy still holding the northern bank of the river including a post 200 yards from site of bridge – this post was heard during the night but except for occasional sniping shots no notice was taken by the enemy.	
			First raft arrived about 3.0 am night of 16/17 – work further hampered by the fact that the roadway of the original bridge consisting of 4" planking bolted & spiked together still lay in the canal & it was impossible to remove it – holes had therefore to be cut to allow trestle legs to pass through.	
	17		Morning broke clear but work continued without interruption from the enemy, except for 1 shell & a few bullets which seemed to indicate that he had not realised the work in hand.	
			Bridge completed by noon but chesses left on bank in order to avoid attracting notice of aeroplanes – span of bridge 60' – depth from roadway to bottom of canal 20'.	
			3 sections 474 Field Co attached to assist this company for the night & were sent up at dusk to lay chesses on canal bridge & get a footbridge across the SOMME river, using piles of old bridge.	
		7.30pm	1 company infantry ferried over river to HALLE, followed by a second company – night footbridge completed – HALLE found unoccupied & infantry pushed on to RADEGONDE & LA QUINCONCE	
	18	8 am	Orders received to carry on making trestle bridge across SOMME & to prepare pontoon raft for ferrying guns & cavalry – trestle sent to site	
		10 am	Pontoons carried over & launched in canal & 20' x 15' pontoon raft (6 section pontoon) commenced. On south bank remains of old pier used as landing stage – new stage erected on north bank.	
			Raft & staging completed by 2.0 PM.	

A5834 Wt. W4973 M687 750,000 8/16 D. D. & L. Ltd. Forms/C.2118/13.

Instructions regarding War Diaries and Intelligence Summaries are contained in F. S. Regs., Part II. and the Staff Manual respectively. Title pages will be prepared in manuscript.

WAR DIARY
or
~~INTELLIGENCE SUMMARY.~~

(*Erase heading not required.*) 475 (SOUTH MIDLAND) FIELD Co RE

Army Form C. 2118.

66

Place	Date	Hour	Summary of Events and Information	Remarks and references to Appendices
	1917			
PRISE	March 18		Gap to be bridged across SOMME 280' - former bridge had been destroyed by explosives & ~~fire~~ burnt but 40' on S bank & 30' on north bank was fairly sound, a few baulks having been cut & piles damaged. Original bridge was on piles & for the greater part of the destroyed portion the majority of these were standing at or about water level. Decided to utilise ~~these~~ piles & build on them. Construction of bridge commenced about noon but work necessarily slow owing to one bay only being capable of repair at a time - work continued all night but difficult owing to very dark night	
	19	7.30am	1 Battery RHA arrived & ferrying commenced	
			By noon ferry had transported 1 Battery RHA & ammunition wagons	
			2 troops Cavalry O.L.O.Y	
			1 platoon cyclists	
			approx 200 infantry in small parties	
			Ferry interfered with bridge construction owing to South end of bridge being used as landing stage -	
		3.30pm	Bridge completed - 4 pontoon superstructure (85') being utilised in centre portion. This was the first bridge for field artillery & horse vehicles constructed across the SOMME	
			News received that 143 Inf Brigade had been the first into PERONNE	
	20		Sections rested	
	21	7.30am	2 Sections sent up to make good footbridge into PERONNE - 2/Lt H R LAMBERT killed & 2 sappers wounded by explosion of mine underwater in gap in one of these footbridges - 3 out of 4 of these bridges were mined by the enemy	
HALLE		2.30pm	Company moved to HALLE - one section quartered at BAZINCOURT FARM for maintenance of bridge which is being used very much by 48 & 40 Dvns ~~the~~ being only access to PERONNE	

A5834 Wt. W4973 M687 750,000 8/16 D. D. & L. Ltd. Forms/C.2118/13.

Instructions regarding War Diaries and Intelligence Summaries are contained in F. S. Regs., Part II. and the Staff Manual respectively. Title pages will be prepared in manuscript.

WAR DIARY
or
INTELLIGENCE SUMMARY.

(*Erase heading not required.*) 475 (SOUTH MIDLAND) FIELD Co RE

Army Form C. 2118.

67

Place	Date	Hour	Summary of Events and Information	Remarks and references to Appendices
	1917 March		Message from CRE - copy message from GOC to ? "The GOC wishes you to inform Major Eberle & those under his command of his satisfaction at the successful carrying out & completion of the bridge at BAZINCOURT which has not only enabled troops of the Division to cross but has assisted the forward movement generally"	
HALLE	22		Two sections working on footbridge at PERONNE I33 A62 to 86 - ~~completion~~	
			One section on footbridge over SOMME near BAZINCOURT FARM	
	23		do - PERONNE footbridge completed	
	24		Two sections on footbridge 1 mile south of PERONNE (O.9.B)	
		10 am	Orders received to start trunk girder bridge over SOMME CANAL at PERONNE	
		noon	Work commenced with above 2 sections - gap 100' - girders to be 40' for 30' gaps, remainder heavy trestles	
			1 section on footbridge at BAZINCOURT	
	25		Crib piers completed & one girder nearly complete - 2 trestles completed	
	26		Girders completed & launching gear ready - sheers on far bank & derrick on near bank	
	27		Morning occupied in launching & getting into position two heavy railway metals 60' long & weighing ½ ton each to act as skids - first girder took 3 hours, second 2 hours	
			Girders launched & got into position - Work continued by artificial light to 10.30 pm	
	28		Launching 3 heavy trestles, concreting abutments & bracing & tying girders, minimum of 1½ in bay	
	29		Laying roadway, consisting of 45lb rails, transoms (girders) of RSJ's 6 x 4 - decking 2 layers of 2" planking	
			Bridge completed except for handrail	
	30	9 am	First 3-ton lorry passed over - deflection of girder only 1/16th inch & this was recovered at once. Bridge calculated to take 12 tons - (8 tons on an axle)	
	31		Completing concreting & clearing up	

G H Eberle Major RE(T)

Vol 25

Confidential

War Diary of
475th (S.M.) Field Company R.E.
for month of
April 1917.

pps 68-69.

Army Form C. 2118.

Instructions regarding War Diaries and Intelligence Summaries are contained in F. S. Regs., Part II. and the Staff Manual respectively. Title pages will be prepared in manuscript.

WAR DIARY
or
~~INTELLIGENCE SUMMARY.~~

(Erase heading not required.) 475 (SOUTH MIDLAND) FIELD Co RE

68

Place	Date	Hour	Summary of Events and Information	Remarks and references to Appendices
PERONNE	1917 April 1		Maintenance of 3 bridges at PERONNE & one at BAZINCOURT FARM Work on formation of new RE Corps dump at LA CHAPELETTE	
	2		do	
	3		do	
	4		do	
	5		do	
	6		do	
	7		do	
	8		Handed over to 427 Field Co 42nd Division	
VILLERS FAUCON	9		Moved forward to VILLERS FAUCON & ST EMILIE	
	10		Work on wells at VILLERS FAUCON reconnoitred siting of Divisional support line behind LEMPIRE & extending to Quarry east of TEMPLEUX	
	11		do - work on support line commenced	
	12		do	
ST EMILIE	13		Headquarters moved from Kite Balloon shed 1 mile west of VILLERS FAUCON to ST EMILIE	
	14		work continued - new line from ST EMILIE southwards sited	
	15		do	
	16		do	
	17		TOMBOIS Fm captured - one section RE & platoon 5 Sussex pioneers consolidated the position - RE doing 160 yards wire - Barbed wire concertina fence.	
	18		work continued	
RONSSOY	19		Moved to RONSSOY - 2 sections & HQ. 2 sections engaged in night operations - attack on the knoll (east of TOMBOIS Farm) & GUILLEMONT FARM failed	
	20		work continued	
	21		Suspension of work on Divisional line (Brown line)	
	22		do	
	23		do - attack on Gillemont Fm - sections attached to Brigade but not used owing to situation not being cleared up before daylight	
	24		do. -	

A5834 Wt. W4973 M687 750,000 8/16 D. D. & L. Ltd. Forms/C.2118/13.

Instructions regarding War Diaries and Intelligence Summaries are contained in F. S. Regs., Part II. and the Staff Manual respectively. Title pages will be prepared in manuscript.

WAR DIARY

or

~~INTELLIGENCE SUMMARY.~~

Army Form C. 2118.

(Erase heading not required.) 475 (SOUTH MIDLAND) FIELD Co RE

69

Place	Date 1917	Hour	Summary of Events and Information	Remarks and references to Appendices
RONSSOY	April 25		Two small strong points constructed North west of GILLEMONT FARM by 1 section RE & 1 platoon pioneers & wired	
	26		Two strong points S W of GILLEMONT Fm dug & wired	
	27		Last named S.Ps extended Two strong points dug & wired east of TOMBOIS Fm in front of outpost line	
	28		General work -	
	29		do - 2 sections RE & 2 platoons pioneers wiring divisional line	
	30		do do.	

[illegible] Major
RE (T)

A5834 Wt. W4973 M687 750,000 8/16 D. D. & L. Ltd. Forms/C.2118/13.

Vol 26

WAR DIARY

of

495th (S.M.) Field Coy R.E.

for month of

MAY 1917.

Apps 70 - 71.

Instructions regarding War Diaries and Intelligence Summaries are contained in F. S. Regs., Part II. and the Staff Manual respectively. Title pages will be prepared in manuscript.

WAR DIARY
or
~~INTELLIGENCE SUMMARY.~~

Army Form C. 2118.

(Erase heading not required.) 475 (SOUTH MIDLAND) FIELD Co RE

70

Place	Date	Hour	Summary of Events and Information	Remarks and references to Appendices
	1917			
RONSSOY	May 1		2 sections moved to BRIE & PERONNE respectively & took over work on roads & control of stone siding at station — 427 Field Co (42 Div.) took over	
			H.Q. moved to ST. EMILIE	
			Communication trench 800x long dug from original front line to GILLEMONT Fm — under supervision of 1 section — parties employed 5 platoon pioneers, 3 sections R.E. & 300 infantry	
			Wiring of Divisional (Brown) Line completed	
ST EMILIE	2		Communication trench deepened to 5' & completed	
			All work handed over to 427 Field Co	
PERONNE	3.		One section moved to MONS-EN-CHAUSSEE for employment on Corps road	
			" " " " TINCOURT " "	
			H.Q. — " PERONNE — maintenance of bridges & general back area work taken over from 42 Div	
	4		General work on Corps roads etc	
	5		do	
	6		do — sections at MONS-EN-CHAUSSEE & TINCOURT withdrawn to PERONNE for inoculation & training	
	7		do — 2 sections inoculated	
	8		do " rested	
	9.		do & training	
	10		do — one section ordered to TINCOURT for new siding to railway	
	11		Company concentrated at PERONNE for move	
LE MESNIL	12		Company marched to LE MESNIL near LE TRANSLOY & bivouaced	

Instructions regarding War Diaries and Intelligence Summaries are contained in F. S. Regs., Part II. and the Staff Manual respectively. Title pages will be prepared in manuscript.

WAR DIARY
or
~~INTELLIGENCE SUMMARY.~~

(Erase heading not required.) 475 (SOUTH MIDLAND) FIELD Co RE

Army Form C. 2118.

71

Place	Date 1917	Hour	Summary of Events and Information	Remarks and references to Appendices
FREMICOURT	May 13		Company marched to FREMICOURT & bivouaced outside village. Arrangement made to take over work & billets of the 11th Div. Engineers	
BEUGNY	14		Company (less 1 section) moved to BEUGNY & took over work & billets of 86th Field Co	
			1 Section " " LE BUCQUIERE " " " 68th " "	
			Small party took over work & camp of reserve Company (67th Field Co)	
			Company work in left sector with 143 Inf Brigade - work taken over consisted entirely of making dugouts	
	15		work continued	
	16		do	
	17		do	
	18		do	
	19		do	
LE BUCQUIERE	20		Company moved to LE BUCQUIERE & bivouaced in gardens - work of same sector continued	
	21		work on dugouts handed over to 474 Field Co	
	22		Wiring (tactical) of brigade reserve line commenced with 2 section RE & 25 infantry - all night work in this sector - 200x entanglement 18' deep constructed on very dark night	
			2 section employed on OPs & general work	
	23		do - 200x wire entanglement	
	24		do 250x " " - new moon began	
	25		do 300x " well at LOUVERVAL (6'x4') commenced	
	26		do 300x	
	27		do - 7 OPs completed - 300x wire	
	28		do 300x wire	
	29		do wiring section rested	
	30		do 300x wire	
	31			

G F [illegible] Major RE (T)

C.R.E.
48th Division

Herewith under Secret Cover. The War Diary of the 475th (S.M.) Field Coy. R.E. for the month of June 1917. Pages 72 and 73.

475TH
(SOUTH MIDLAND)
FIELD COMPANY, R.E.
No. ✓
Date July 1st.

Captain
for MAJOR, R. E.
Comdg, 475, (S.M.) Field Coy.
P.P.

Instructions regarding War Diaries and Intelligence Summaries are contained in F. S. Regs., Part II. and the Staff Manual respectively. Title pages will be prepared in manuscript.

WAR DIARY
or
INTELLIGENCE SUMMARY.
(Erase heading not required.)

Army Form C. 2118.

475 (S.M.) Field Coy R.E. 72

Place	Date 1917	Hour	Summary of Events and Information	Remarks and references to Appendices
LEBUCQUIERE	1st June		Maj G. F. Eberle O.C. Coy proceeds to 48th Div. C.R.E.'s Office for one month's course. 2 Secs continue wiring Intermediate (HERMIES-DOIGNIES) Line. 2 Secs employed on O.P.'s, sinking well at LOUVERVAL, cross country night tracks.	
	2nd		Do. O.P.'s in left 3rd Sector completed.	
	3rd		Do	
	4th		Do. Digging of Posts in Intermediate Line carried out by Inf labour.	
	5th		Do	
	6th		Do. Tracks completed.	
	7th		Inf Relief Day. Coy employed in training	
	8th		Do. Work continued & 1 Sec employed on new screened route from LOUVERVAL to BOURSIES.	
	9th		Do. 4 Stag ricks erected on 144 Inf Bde transport lines	
	10		Do. 2 Secs on Intermediate Line employed on digging posts	
	11		Do. Screened valley route to LOUVERVAL started	
	12		Do. Making up of trestles for future bridging operations started.	
	13		Do.	
	14		Do. 2 Secs on Intermediate Line employed on strengthening Defensive wire.	
	15		Do. New Divl O.P. dugout started	

A5834 Wt. W4973 M687 750,000 8/16 D. D. & L. Ltd. Forms/C.2118/13.

Army Form C. 2118.

WAR DIARY
or
~~INTELLIGENCE SUMMARY.~~
(Erase heading not required.)

Instructions regarding War Diaries and Intelligence Summaries are contained in F. S. Regs., Part II. and the Staff Manual respectively. Title pages will be prepared in manuscript.

475 (S.M.) Field Coy. R.E. 73.

Vol 27

Place	Date 1917	Hour	Summary of Events and Information	Remarks and references to Appendices
LEBUCQUIERE	16 June	Do.	Divl. O.P. Dugout completed. Supervision of A & C Coys. 5th R. Sussex Regt. working on intermediate line on Posts & Dugouts.	
	17 "	Do.		
	18	Do.		
	19	Do.	O.P. for R.A at J5c72 strengthened & new entrance to dug out started	
	20	Do.	Screened Valley Route to LOUVERVAL completed as far as Intermediate (Line	
			Repair & Drainage of BAPAUME-CAMBRAI Road started	
	21	Do.	Bombing Course for Company started, two days for each Section	
	22	Do.	Petrol Pump (6000 galls per hr) placed in position in chamber of well at depth of 57 feet. (LOUVERVAL Well)	
	23	Do.		
	24	Do.		
	25	Do.	6 Trestles completed.	
	26	Do.		
	27	Do.	Section Bombing courses completed	
	28	Do.		
	29	Do.		
	30	Do.	Maj. G. F. Eberle O.C. Coy. rejoins	

G F Eberle Major RE

A5834 Wt. W4973 M687 750,000 8/16 D. D. & L. Ltd. Forms/C.2118/13.

Vol 28

Confidential.

War Diary of

475th (S.M.) Field Company R.E.

for month of

July 1917.

Vol 28
Sheets 1, 2 and 3.

Instructions regarding War Diaries and Intelligence Summaries are contained in F. S. Regs., Part II. and the Staff Manual respectively. Title pages will be prepared in manuscript.

WAR DIARY
or
~~INTELLIGENCE SUMMARY.~~ 475 (S.M.) Field Coy R.E.

(*Erase heading not required.*)

Army Form C. 2118.

74

Place	Date 1917	Hour	Summary of Events and Information	Remarks and references to Appendices
LEBUCQUIÈRE	1st July		All work handed over to 456th Field Coy R.E.	
ACHIET LE PETIT	2nd	2 pm	Coy move to ACHIET LE PETIT & occupy R.E. Camp on outskirts of Village. Move complete by 6.30 pm	
	3rd		Coy Training – Drill – Physical Exercises. Bayonet Fighting etc	
	4th		Do	
	5th		Coy marched to ACHIET LE GRAND & entrained in two halves. First half leaving at 4 pm, second half 8 pm	
A 24 d 11	6th		Coy detrained at HOPOUTRE & marched via POPERINGHE to wood in A 24 d 11 a bivouacked for night.	Ref MAP BELGIUM Sheet 28 NW Ed 5a 1/20,000
	7th		Coy Training – Musketry. Bayonet Fighting, Physical Exercises	
		3 pm	Camp shelled 5 O.R. wounded & 19 Horses disabled	
		11 pm	Coy moved to E Camp in A 30 a	
			Maj. G.P. Elwell leaves for England to attend Senior Officers Course.	
A 30 a	8th	6.30 pm	Coy less bridging wagons march to L Camp on POPERINGHE – WATOU Road.	
L Camp.	9th		Coy Resting	
	10th		Do Reconnaissance of forward area.	
	11th	3 pm	Nos 1 & 2 Secs march to forward billet in BURGOMASTER FARM H 5 b less mounted portion of Sections. No 1 Sec takes over work on construction of shelters in bank of YPERLEE Stream from E. Yorks Pioneers. No 2 Sec employed on improvement of accomodation in billets	

A5834 Wt. W4973 M687 750,000 8/16 D. D. & L. Ltd. Forms/C.2118/13.

Army Form C. 2118.

WAR DIARY
or
INTELLIGENCE SUMMARY.

(Erase heading not required.)

Instructions regarding War Diaries and Intelligence Summaries are contained in F. S. Regs., Part II. and the Staff Manual respectively. Title pages will be prepared in manuscript.

475 (S.M.) Field Coy R.E. VOL 28 Sheet 1. 75

Place	Date 1917	Hour	Summary of Events and Information	Remarks and references to Appendices
L Camp	12th July		Capt J.R.M. Crawford from 477 (S.M.) Field Coy RE assumes command of Coy	Ref Map BELGIUM 28 N.W. Edn 5a 1/20,000
Camp at A 21 a 87		12.45pm	Remainder of Coy march to camp at A 21 a 87. Move completed by 7.30 pm	
			No 3 Sec employed in making camouflage at 39' Dw. RE Dump	
	13th		Nos 1, 2, & 3 Secs. continue work as above. No 4 Sec employed on camp improvements	
	14th		Do	
	15th		Do	
	16th	6pm	No 3 Sec march to new billet in Canal Bank in C 25 a 86. Nos 1 & 2 Secs move to same billets. Nos 1 & 2 Sections continue work as above	TRENCH MAP ST JULIEN 28 N.W. 2 Ed 5A 1.10.000
	18		Work continued on shelters in bank of YPERLEE. Owing to small height of bank & bad design in the original excavations as handed over these shelters could not be made into a satisfactory job, but in all accomodation for 120 men was provided.	
	19.		No 2 section were detailed to help 477 Field Co in cutting a track through Canal Bank opposite bridge 2A. It was proposed to carry this track through to our front line via IRISH FARM & HILL TOP.	

A5834 Wt. W4973 M687 750,000 8/16 D. D. & L. Ltd. Forms/C.2118/13.

Army Form C. 2118.

WAR DIARY
or
~~INTELLIGENCE SUMMARY.~~
(Erase heading not required.)

Instructions regarding War Diaries and Intelligence Summaries are contained in F. S. Regs., Part II. and the Staff Manual respectively. Title pages will be prepared in manuscript.

VOL 28 sheet 2.

Place	Date	Hour	Summary of Events and Information	Remarks and references to Appendices
[illegible]	JULY 20.		No4 section relieved No1. An existing well at I 1 b 08 was taken in hand & cleaned out. It was proposed to place wooden cover over the top, bolt pump thereon & fix up a tank, the whole job being sandbagged up. Remainder of section were employed on screens between C 19 d 93 & C 19 d 55. This work & also that on the track from Bridge 2A was very considerably interfered with by enemy shelling with a new form of gas shell which caused many casualties. The effect was generally felt about 12-24 hours after the event being chiefly confined to intense irritation of the eyes, nose & throat though occasionally those who had come in contact with gas impregnated earth suffered from large blisters even through their clothing.	TRENCH MAP. ST JULIEN 28 N.W. 2 Ed 5 A. 1.10.000.
	22.		Capt V. F. EBERLE left the unit to become adjutant to CRE 48th Div. Little work was able to be done owing to the enemy practice of putting down intense barrages of gas shells along the line of the CANAL. Casualties were now becoming serious, the 3 sections in the line being reduced to an effective strength of only 63.	

A5834 Wt. W4973 M687 750,000 8/16 D. D. & L. Ltd. Forms/C.2118/13.

Instructions regarding War Diaries and Intelligence Summaries are contained in F. S. Regs., Part II. and the Staff Manual respectively. Title pages will be prepared in manuscript.

WAR DIARY
or
~~INTELLIGENCE SUMMARY.~~
(*Erase heading not required.*)

Army Form C. 2118.

VOL 28 sheet 3

Place	Date	Hour	Summary of Events and Information	Remarks and references to Appendices
	JULY. 25.		The 3 sections in the line returned to HQ at A 21 a 87. their respective strengths being No1 - 33. No 2 - 18, - No 3 - 18, No4 - 26, inclusive of all details such as cooks, orderlies, tailors saddlers etc.	
	26 27	}	No 1 Section employed on Carpentry work for D.H.Q. Nos 2 3 & 4 Sections rested.	
	28		52 Reinforcements joined the Company, - this number being the allotment record out of 139. Carpentry work for D.H.Q. Continued	TRENCH MAP ST JULIEN 28NW 2 8d5a 1.10 000
	29		Reinforcements practiced in anti gas drill (box respirator) remainder of Company resting & Carpentry work for D.H.Q.	
	30		Dismounted Sections moved to forward Camp ~~H 20~~ H 4C under Major Crawford leaving at 3.30 P.M. Transport & Mounted Section remained at Camp (A 21 a 87)	
	31		Forward Sections stood by awaiting orders	

J. W. Bassatt Lieut
for MAJOR, R. E.
Comdg, 475, (S.M.) Field Coy.

A5834 Wt. W4973/M687 750,000 8/16 D. D. & L. Ltd. Forms/C.2118/13.

Vol 29

CONFIDENTIAL

WAR DIARY

of

475th (South Midland) Field Coy. R.E. (T.F.)

From 1st August 1917 to 31st August 1917.

Army Form C. 2118.

WAR DIARY
or
~~INTELLIGENCE~~ SUMMARY.
(Erase heading not required.)

Instructions regarding War Diaries and Intelligence Summaries are contained in F. S. Regs., Part II. and the Staff Manual respectively. Title pages will be prepared in manuscript.

VOL 29 sheet 1.

Place	Date	Hour	Summary of Events and Information	Remarks and references to Appendices
VLAMERTINGHE.	Aug 1		Camp was annoyed all night by 4.2 HV gun which fired with some frequency & not a little accuracy. 6 casualties during the day, mostly light. Stood by the whole day. Reconnoitred ADMIRALS ROAD with a view to getting traffic through to Northern Div Boundary near MORTELDGE ESTAMINET.	
	2.	4.0 AM	Work started on ADMIRALS ROAD using 2 sections. Clearing mud & grass off road surface & digging drains. Road surface fair considering that it had been in No Mans Land for over 2 years but large quantity of shell holes.	PILCKEM. ED 1. 1/10.000. and TRENCH MAP ST JULIEN 28 N.W. 2 Edition 5a 1/10.000
	4.		Work continued on ADMIRALS ROAD, 640x cleared & made passable for traffic. HV shells still continued to annoy the camp though no casualties were caused more by good luck than judgement	
	5	4.30 pm.	Handed over camp work to 227 Field CoRE, taking over their billets in CANAL BANK at C 25 d 14.	
CANAL BANK	7.		Work continued on HILLTOP FARM dugouts & trenches outside. Dugouts were full of water owing to slackness on part of previous occupants the trenches had been allowed to get into a very bad state of repair & had also received a good many direct hits	

A5834 Wt. W4973 M687 750,000 8/16 D. D. & L. Ltd. Forms/C.2118/13.

Instructions regarding War Diaries and Intelligence Summaries are contained in F. S. Regs., Part II. and the Staff Manual respectively. Title pages will be prepared in manuscript.

WAR DIARY
or
~~INTELLIGENCE SUMMARY.~~
(Erase heading not required.)

Army Form C. 2118.

Vol. 29 sheet 2

Place	Date	Hour	Summary of Events and Information	Remarks and references to Appendices
CANAL BANK C 25 d 1.4	8		Work continued: 2 sections were put at the disposal 411 Fd Co for work on tram line from site of new Div RE Dump at C 15 a 51 running N of KULTUR FARM, thence to OBLONG FARM.	PILCKEM Edition 1 1/10 000.
	9.		Work on HILLTOP had to be stopped owing to preparations for an offensive which necessitated a large number of small jobs being got on with. 2 sections on tram track were detailed for overland tracks.	
	12		VAN HEULE FARM & CHEDDER VILLA were protected by sandbag walls on enemy side & various fittings made for use as a Brigade HQ. 6 footbridges were made here for crossing the STEENBEEK S of St JULIAN to the southern Div Boundary at C18 c 08. 6 footbridges were also made at ALBERTA from timber taken from old German stores to be used in crossing STEENBEEK from C12 c 15 to northern Div Boundary at C5 d 03. Forward dumps were formed at CORNER COT - KITCHENERS WOOD - C17 a 17. - filled by Pack Transport Co. Very great difficulty was experienced in getting stores up owing to enemy shelling which was generally very accurate, causing nightly casualties to men & animals.	
	14.		Work continued on above jobs & also taped tracks for infantry from ADMIRALS ROAD forward.	

A5834 Wt. W4973 M687 750,000 8/16 D. D. & L. Ltd. Forms/C.2118/13.

Instructions regarding War Diaries and Intelligence Summaries are contained in F. S. Regs., Part II. and the Staff Manual respectively. Title pages will be prepared in manuscript.

WAR DIARY
or
INTELLIGENCE SUMMARY.
(Erase heading not required.)

Army Form C. 2118.

Vol 29 Sheet 3.

Place	Date	Hour	Summary of Events and Information	Remarks and references to Appendices
CANAL BANK.	15.	12 midnight	Dismounted portion of company left for the BUND - C11c98 - where it would remain until the infantry had reached their objectives then construct 5 strong points ① MON DU HIBOU. ② HILLOCK FARM - C12c55. ③ SPRINGFIELD ④ WINNIPEG & ⑤ JEWS HILL - C12 a 22. For this purpose 1 section from 477 Fd Co & 5 platoons 5th Royal Sussex (Pioneers) were attached. The BUND was reached with only 1 casualty to the sappers but instead of finding the place empty reserved for us it was nearly filled with infantry, machine gunners & ?ments. Owing to the darkness & the rough going it took some little time getting in. Just after all the sections had got in & the Sussex in rear arrived the enemy put down a heavy barrage on the line REGINA X - ALBERTA - CORNER COT. Unfortunately it was some time before all the Sussex could get in owing to the crowd of unauthorised people already in the BUND.	PILCKEM Edition 1 1/10.000.
BUND	16		After zero hour 4.45 am - no news could be got until 8.30 am when reconnaissance made plain the fact that our infantry had been held up everywhere except on the extreme right & that the first objectives in front of SPs 1-2 were still in enemy hands. SP No 5 was able to be started by the section of 477 Fd Co. the officer	

A5834 Wt. W4973 M687 750,000 8/16 D. D. & L. Ltd. Forms/C.2118/13.

Instructions regarding War Diaries and Intelligence Summaries are contained in F. S. Regs., Part II. and the Staff Manual respectively. Title pages will be prepared in manuscript.

WAR DIARY
or
~~INTELLIGENCE SUMMARY~~.
(Erase heading not required.)

Army Form C. 2118.

Vol. 29 sheet 5.

Place	Date	Hour	Summary of Events and Information	Remarks and references to Appendices
	22		BATH ROAD continued, also pumping & cleaning old dugouts in German front & second lines. These were all concrete pillboxes mostly undamaged but in an indescribable state of filth & water.	ST JULIEN 6a 1/10.000
	26		All outside jobs were stopped & work concentrated on trench board tracks from CANAL BANK, forward to ALBERTA & No 2 Track; latter ran from ADMIRALS ROAD at C22c95 north of MOUSETRAP & JULIET to a point about C11d53.	
	27	3pm	Zero arranged for 2pm.⊗ Previous to this hour 1 Co 5th R Sussex had been attached for work. 2 sections RE & 2 platoons Sussex carried trenchboards from ADMIRALS ROAD dump to small dumps in CALF RESERVE at C16c94 & C22b59. When the situation cleared at about 5.30pm, these parties carried forward & laid from track head. Work was left at dark, ALBERTA track head then being at C11c98 & No 2 track at C11d9555. Work was continued at dawn using remaining 2 sections & 2 platoons. Very great difficulty was experienced in laying over the broken ground, it was an extreme rarity to get 2 consecutive lengths of trenchboards lying in the same direction, the total distance covered being at least 3 times the actual distance in a straight line.	

⊗ 1.55pm. [illegible]

A5834 Wt. W4973 M687 750,000 8/16 D. D. & L. Ltd. Forms/C.2118/13.

Instructions regarding War Diaries and Intelligence Summaries are contained in F. S. Regs., Part II. and the Staff Manual respectively. Title pages will be prepared in manuscript.

WAR DIARY
or
INTELLIGENCE SUMMARY.
(Erase heading not required.)

Army Form C. 2118.

Vol 29 sheet 6.

Place	Date	Hour	Summary of Events and Information	Remarks and references to Appendices
	27.	cont	When works stopped ALBERTA track head was at C 11 b 4585 & No 2 track at C 12c 38.	
	29		All work in hand was handed over to 511 Field Co.	
			HQ & sappers moved to horse lines to	
	30.		Work started on St JULIEN road from CROSS ROADS FARM to road junction at C 23 a.	
			Some work had already been done by Pioneers but most of this work had been nullified by the zeal of the Tanks who apparently used the formation as a parade ground not without detriment to the timber roadway	

STRENGTH OF COMPANY

				Reinforcements		Killed		CCS		Transfers	
		OFF.	OR.	OFF.	OR.	OFF	OR	TO.	FROM.	TO.	FROM.
Week ending Aug	3.	8	240	-	54	-	2	15	1	1	
	10	7	227	-	-	-	-	13	-	1	-
	17	6	224	-	18	-	2	19	-	1	-
	24	6	220	-	-	-	2	3	1	-	-
	31	7	217	1	-	-	-	3	-	-	-

[illegible] Major
OC 475 Field Coy RE

A5834 Wt. W4973/M687 750,000 8/16 D. D. & L. Ltd. Forms/C.2118/13.

Vol 30

C O N F I D E N T I A L

****

W A R   D I A R Y

o f

475th (South Midland) Field Company R.E.

(Volume 30)

Instructions regarding War Diaries and Intelligence Summaries are contained in F. S. Regs., Part II. and the Staff Manual respectively. Title pages will be prepared in manuscript.

WAR DIARY
or
~~INTELLIGENCE SUMMARY~~.
(Erase heading not required.)

Army Form C. 2118.

VOL 30 Sheet 1

Place	Date	Hour	Summary of Events and Information	Remarks and references to Appendices
BRISTOL FARM. H10c76	Sept 1.		Work continued on St JULIAN road. Beech slabs were not obtainable in sufficient quantity to make good progress possible, owing to wet weather heavy traffic during the last week of August, great difficulties were experienced in making good the formation.	
	4.		Better progress was now being made on the St JULIAN road, fine weather & a more ample supply of material making this possible. A small party was put on to work forward of CALIFORNIA SUPPORT in the early morning. Right side of road was now complete single width up to CALIFORNIA SUPPORT, the road beyond being passable for transport with care.	St JULIAN 28 NW2. Ed 5A. 1/10.000.
	7.		60% of the whole length of road from X ROADS FARM to CALIFORNIA SUPPORT was decked double width & 92x single width E of CALIFORNIA SUPPORT towards the road junction at C 23 a 52.	
			Major Crawford went on leave.	

Army Form C. 2118.

Instructions regarding War Diaries and Intelligence Summaries are contained in F. S. Regs., Part II. and the Staff Manual respectively. Title pages will be prepared in manuscript.

WAR DIARY
or
~~INTELLIGENCE~~ SUMMARY.
(Erase heading not required.)

Vol 30 sheet 2.

Place	Date	Hour	Summary of Events and Information	Remarks and references to Appendices
BRISTOL FARM.	SEPT 10.		Handed over work on road to 2 Coy 5th R Sussex. Since Aug 31st. 1611x of road had been made, including draining, making formation, laying bearers & decking etc. When handed over timber road was within 180x of road junction at C 23 a 52, practically the entire length from X Roads Farm being double width.	St JULIEN 28 N.W.2 Ed. 6a 1/10,000
	13.		Company training. Drill, map reading, use of the compass etc etc being carried out. Several small jobs were also taken in hand, 3 elephant shelters on E bank of CANAL about C 25 b 11 being repaired & 2200x camouflage on wire netting salved & made. Various improvements made to billets in BRISTOL FARM including drying room for mens clothes, cookhouse, ablution sheds.	
	19.		Company training continued. Major Crawford returned from leave. Site of stables at H6 c 02 taken over from 504 Fd CoRE	
	23.		Work on stables continued. Lack of materials made progress impossible. When materials did come up they were generally inadequate.	
	27.		Moved to billets on E CANAL BANK took over work of 504 Field CoRE. Horse lines moved to H 36 near MARSH FARM.	

Instructions regarding War Diaries and Intelligence Summaries are contained in F. S. Regs., Part II. and the Staff Manual respectively. Title pages will be prepared in manuscript.

WAR DIARY
or
~~INTELLIGENCE SUMMARY.~~
(Erase heading not required.)

Army Form C. 2118.

VOL 30. Sheet 3.

Place	Date	Hour	Summary of Events and Information	Remarks and references to Appendices
	Sept 27 contd		Work consisted of repair & extension of trenchboard tracks running E from CANAL BANK. ALBERTA AVENUE to ALBERTA & MON DU HIBOU & MOUSETRAP AVENUE to MOUSETRAP FARM & SPRINGFIELD. These were the same tracks as handed over by us, but maintenance & repair had been very much neglected with the result that large portions of both tracks had become unuseable owing to wear & shell fire.	ST JULIEN 28 N.W. 2 Ed 5a. 1/10.000.
CANAL BANK.	28		Work continued on tracks, 1 section with platoon Sussex Pioneers working on each track up to STEENBEEK with section of platoon forward.	
	29.		Forward sections of platoons turned on to a tramline for battery positions on STEENBEEK. This tramline ran from C 5 d 0000 to C 1 b 6028, a total distance of 487x. Formation was completed.	
	30.		Practically the entire length of line was laid on wooden sleepers & ballasted. 2 switches being taken off to supply battery positions direct. 2110x trenchboard track taken up, relaid on bearers & repaired.	

A5834 Wt. W4973/M687 750,000 8/16 D. D. & L. Ltd. Forms/C.2118/13.

Army Form C. 2118.

Instructions regarding War Diaries and Intelligence Summaries are contained in F. S. Regs., Part II. and the Staff Manual respectively. Title pages will be prepared in manuscript.

WAR DIARY
or
~~INTELLIGENCE SUMMARY.~~
(Erase heading not required.)

VOL 30. Sheet 4

Place	Date	Hour	Summary of Events and Information	Remarks and references to Appendices
			STRENGTH OF COMPANY.	

Week ending	Off.	OR.	Reinforcements Off	Reinforcements OR	Killed	CCS To	CCS From	Transfers To	Transfers From
Sept 7.	7	217	-	2	-	1	-	1	-
14	7	218	-	1	1	5	5	-	-
21	7	207	-	-	-	11	-	-	-
28	7	204	-	-	-	4	1	-	-

Actual Strength Sept 28th.

OFF.	OR.
6.	184

Detached

	OFF	OR.
Hospital	-	10.
Leave	-	2.
CRE: office	1	2.
ASC.	-	1
Div RE store	-	5
	1.	20.

T. R. McCrawford
Major
OC. 473 Field CoRE.

A5834 Wt. W4973 M687 750,000 8/16 D. D. & L. Ltd. Forms/C.2118/13.

Instructions regarding War Diaries and Intelligence Summaries are contained in F. S. Regs., Part II. and the Staff Manual respectively. Title pages will be prepared in manuscript.

WAR DIARY
or
~~INTELLIGENCE SUMMARY.~~
(Erase heading not required.)

Army Form C. 2118.

Vol. 29 sheet 4

Place	Date	Hour	Summary of Events and Information	Remarks and references to Appendices
	16. cont'd		Lt Cubitt, showing commendable initiative & resource. The position remained the same until 5pm when orders came through to consolidate JEWS HILL, HILLOCK FARM & BORDER HOUSE. 2 sections RE & 2 platoons Pioneers were detailed for the last each of these positions as it was obvious from direct observation that HILLOCK FARM was still in enemy hands. The BORDER HOUSE party returned, reporting that our infantry did not hold this position but the JEWS HILL ~~—~~ point was dug further & wired. On completion the whole party returned to billets on CANAL BANK	ST JULIEN 28 N.W. 2 Edition 6a 1/10.000
CANAL BANK.	18		Work was started on BATH ROAD – a fair weather track from ADMIRALS ROAD at C 22 a 13 to OBLONG FARM & ALBERTA. Owing to wet weather & heavy shelling this track was in an appalling condition, but large parties were not possible owing to the enemy having observation on it.	
	20.		Work on BATH ROAD continued. During the evening forming up tapes were laid from a point C 12 d 0 2 to C 12 a 6 4. The ground between these two points was badly cut up & some places under water for long stretches, making diversions necessary. In all 1600x was laid out.	

A5834 Wt. W4973 M687 750,000 8/16 D. D. & L. Ltd. Forms/C.2118/13.

Vol 31

C O N F I D E N T I A L

W A R D I A R Y

O F

475th (South Midland) Field Co. R.E.

From 1st October 1917 to 31st October 1917.

(Volume 31)

Army Form C. 2118.

Instructions regarding War Diaries and Intelligence Summaries are contained in F. S. Regs., Part II. and the Staff Manual respectively. Title pages will be prepared in manuscript.

WAR DIARY
or
~~INTELLIGENCE SUMMARY.~~
(Erase heading not required.)

Vol. 31. [illegible] 1

Place	Date	Hour	Summary of Events and Information	Remarks and references to Appendices
CANAL BANK	Oct 1		Tramline was completed over entire length with 3 junctions to battery positions & trenchboards laid on wood bearers along whole length. Trenchboards tracks were also relaid on bearers; MOUSETRAP 680x & ALBERTA 2000x.	St JULIEN 28 N.W.2 Ed. 6a 1/10,000
	3		Steel [illegible] was now being [illegible] on the extension of trenchboard tracks forward. It was recognised by all ranks that the laying of these tracks was the only practicable means of communication towards the front line, even though boards were not laid on a formation. In the present state of the ground it is impossible for men to progress other than on the tracks. On MOUSETRAP 590x were laid from SPRINGFIELD to 60x SW of ARBRE & 519x on ALBERTA, track head being C6 a 3525(?)	
	4		Trenchboard tracks continued. MOUSETRAP track head at D7 a 34. ALBERTA at D7 c 4032(?)	
	5		MOUSETRAP track head D7 b 2868; ALBERTA D7 d 2368. On the latter track 130x had to be completely relaid owing to infantry transport using trenchboards for pack transport in preference to roads to HUBNER.	

A5834 Wt. W4973 M687 750,000 8/16 D. D. & L. Ltd. Forms/C.2118/13.

Army Form C. 2118.

Instructions regarding War Diaries and Intelligence Summaries are contained in F. S. Regs., Part II. and the Staff Manual respectively. Title pages will be prepared in manuscript.

WAR DIARY
or
INTELLIGENCE SUMMARY.
(Erase heading not required.)

Vol. 31 sheet 2.

Place	Date	Hour	Summary of Events and Information	Remarks and references to Appendices
CANAL BANK	Oct 6.		MOUSETRAP track head at D7 b 6595: ALBERTA at D1 d 4585. All existing tracks were maintained, slats being repaired, shell holes repaired, formation gradually completed. 3 Bridges were placed across the STROOMBEEK at D1 d 48, D2c 4575, D2c 6573.	
	7	10am	Summer time ceased. Tracks continued with varying success, owing to delays, non-arrival of transport & hostile shelling. Owing to numerous gun positions on TRIANGLE – ST JULIEN ROAD with the consequent supply of ammunition, it was practically impossible to get material up to the dump at TRIANGLE E	
	8		Work concentrated on ALBERTA. 400x laid, track head being at D1 b 9575. It is necessary at this point to draw attention to the work of the RE & carrying parties of Pioneers & Infantry. They all had a 4 miles march to the most advanced possible position for a dump at TRIANGLE E. Owing to small size of party it was necessary to do 3 journeys to track head with a trenchboard each time. This distance was 1½ miles & a trenchboard weighs 30 odd pounds. 3 journeys of 3 miles & 2 journeys of 4 miles makes 17 miles daily, a task which they	

A5834 Wt. W4973 M687 750,000 8/16 D. D. & L. Ltd. Forms/C.2118/13.

Instructions regarding War Diaries and Intelligence Summaries are contained in F. S. Regs., Part II. and the Staff Manual respectively. Title pages will be prepared in manuscript.

WAR DIARY
or
~~INTELLIGENCE~~ SUMMARY.
(*Erase heading not required.*)

Army Form C. 2118.

Vol 31 sheet 3.

Place	Date	Hour	Summary of Events and Information	Remarks and references to Appendices
CANAL BANK	8		performed under – at times – heavy shell fire, always in the dark, on an uneven track & generally in the rain. In my opinion the work was an example of quite endurance on the part of all ranks was the direct cause of saving many wounded who would otherwise have perished in the mud owing to the impossibility of their being brought back.	
	9		An attempt by was made to continue work on ALBERTA during daylight but party was promptly shelled off though work was persisted in little progress was made.	
	10		Work in hand turned over to 64 Field Coy RE During the second period in the line 3564x of entirely new track was laid & 8605x old track repaired, taken up & laid on bearers, a total of 12169x or about 7 miles. It must be remembered that the sappers had been continuously at work since July 17th under very adverse conditions, heavy casualties, shelled on the work, bombed & shelled when in billets. For all ranks the entire time had been very strenuous & nerve racking	

A5834 Wt. W4973 M687 750,000 8/16 D. D. & L. Ltd. Forms/C.2118/13.

Army Form C. 2118.

Instructions regarding War Diaries and Intelligence Summaries are contained in F. S. Regs., Part II. and the Staff Manual respectively. Title pages will be prepared in manuscript.

WAR DIARY
or
INTELLIGENCE SUMMARY.
(Erase heading not required.)

Vol 31 sheet 4

Place	Date	Hour	Summary of Events and Information	Remarks and references to Appendices
CANAL BANK	10 cont'd		Whole company moved back to camp at A 22 b 55	TRENCH MAP BELGIUM 28 N.W. Ed 6a 1/20,000.
A22 b 55.	14.	2.0 am	Company entrained at PESELHOEK, leaving at 5.0 am.	
	15.	1.0 pm	Arrived MAROEUIL proceeded to billets at ACQ.	FRANCE Ed 2. LENS 11 1/100,000
	19.	10 am	Moved to AUX RIETZ & took over work from 5th Canadian Fd Coy R.E.	
	18		Work generally consisted of trench upkeep, overland tracks etc. Company worked with 144 Inf Brigade on the left. Trenches when we took over were in fair condition throughout, mostly trenchboarded but very narrow with vertical sides. The first work was to trim throughout & clear back sides to 3/1 slope. The distances were very great & the trenches generally were made for 'push' purposes only & were not intended for winter use.	LENS [illegible] 1/20,000
			3 sections moved into billets at PETIT VIMY at S 24 b 52, HQ, horselines & 1 section at AUX RIETZ at 8 c 56	ROCLINCOURT Ed 6a Sheet 51 B N.W. 1/10,000

A5834 Wt. W4973 M687 750,000 8/16 D. D. & L. Ltd. Forms/C.2118/13.

Army Form C. 2118.

Vol 31 sheet 5

WAR DIARY

or

~~INTELLIGENCE SUMMARY.~~

(Erase heading not required.)

Instructions regarding War Diaries and Intelligence Summaries are contained in F. S. Regs., Part II. and the Staff Manual respectively. Title pages will be prepared in manuscript.

Place	Date	Hour	Summary of Events and Information	Remarks and references to Appendices
Av. [illegible]	20.		Work was completed on HAYTER as far as [illegible] & WHITE TRAIL. [illegible] was an [illegible] track running from Lens - ARRAS ROAD at S13 d 2532 to HAYTER TUNNEL at T13 b57, a total distance of 1220.x Work on HAYTER was [illegible] back to 3 [illegible] to 5/1 [illegible], digging sumps & draining.	TRENCH TRACINGS 1/10 000.
	22.		[illegible] for WHITE TRAIL was completed over whole length. 6 sumps started on HAYTER, whole length of trench was [illegible] to 3' & 5 [illegible] [illegible] [illegible] B.R's [illegible]	
	24.		WHITE TRAIL completed with trenchboards, trench bridges & steps. The [illegible] of HAYTER TUNNEL was taken in hand so as [illegible] the approach on the E side of railway Embankment. This meant a 23' gallery & [illegible] frames & filling in at the junction with existing gallery.	
	2[illegible].		Work on HAYTER was progressing well. KEANE had also been [illegible] along the whole length. [illegible] showed little apparent progress as all spoil from sides [illegible] had to be thrown on berm & cleared nightly.	

A5834 Wt. W4973 M687 750,000 8/16 D. D. & L. Ltd. Forms/C.2118/13.

Instructions regarding War Diaries and Intelligence Summaries are contained in F. S. Regs., Part II. and the Staff Manual respectively. Title pages will be prepared in manuscript.

WAR DIARY
or
INTELLIGENCE SUMMARY.
(Erase heading not required.)

Army Form C. 2118.

Vol 31 sheet 6.

Place	Date	Hour	Summary of Events and Information	Remarks and references to Appendices
[illegible]	29		HAYTER TUNNEL completed. RE dump at VICTORIA now looking like a store, large quantities of RE material being nightly brought up by railway. Work on all trenches progresses fairly smoothly. This work was started only just in time, just making to appearance that now means rain at times. If weather continues as at present up to the [illegible] there is a chance of making trenches sufficiently [illegible] to hold the winter [illegible] in any case is hopeless, being very narrow trenches.	TRENCH TRACINGS 1/10,000
	31.		Work continued on trenches. 7 pumps were completed to depth on HAYTER average dimension 11' x 11' x 11'. These will be frames revetted the connecting drains ducked. Pumps started off KEANE	

31/10/17.

H. M. Crawford Major

OC 475 Field CoRE

A5834 Wt. W4973 M687 750,000 8/16 D. D. & L. Ltd. Forms/C.2118/13.

www.ingramcontent.com/pod-product-compliance
Lightning Source LLC
Chambersburg PA
CBHW081544160426
43191CB00011B/1835
* 9 7 8 1 4 7 4 5 2 6 7 1 5 *